Proficiency PASSKEY
Workbook

NICK KENNY

**MACMILLAN
HEINEMANN**
English Language Teaching

Macmillan Heinemann English Language Teaching
Macmillan Oxford, Between Towns Road, Oxford OX4 PP
A division of Macmillan Publishers Limited

Companies and representatives throughout the world

ISBN 0 333 75508 1 (with key)
      0 333 75612 6 (without key)

Text © Nick Kenny 1999
Design © Macmillan Publishers Limited 1999
Heinemann is a registered trademark of Reed Educational and Professional Publishing Limited

First published 1999

All rights reserved; no part of this publication may be reproduced, stored in a retrieval system, transmitted in any form, or by any means, electronic, mechanical, photocopying, recording, or otherwise, without the prior written permission of the publishers.

Designed by Giles Davies
Illustrated by Kingsley Wiggin

Acknowledgements

The author and publishers would like to thank Jean Kennedy, Barbara Lewis and David Oakley for their help and support.

The author and publishers wish to thank the following for kindly granting permission to quote from copyright work: Bob Carter for his story 'On four legs you can take forever', pp89–90; Noonie Coldrey for an extract adapted from 'Little Venice', p95; Concept Plublishing for extracts adapted from 'Flocking back to nature', p42 and 'Our blue period', p66 (*Welcome Aboard* Magazine, April/May 1998); The Conde Nast Publications Limited for an extract adapted from 'Candid Counsel' by Julia Samuel, p39 (*The Tatler*. July 1998, © Tatler/Conde Nast Publications Limited); Guardian News Service Limited for the article 'Let's not fight about it' by Deborah Tannen, pp68–69 (*The Guardian* 1 January 1998), and the article 'Mind your language' by Bill Saunders, pp25–26 (*The Observer*, 18 March 1996); David Higham Associates on behalf of Dorothy L. Sayers for an extract from *Gaudy Night*, pp76–77, (HarperCollins Publishers Limited); The Illustrated London News Picture Library for an extract adapted from *Scarves as Works of Art* by Sharon Maxwell p64 (No. 10, 1987); Independent Newspapers (UK) Limited for extracts from the article 'The world is just a great big tortellone' by Keith Batsford, p6 (*The Independent* 5 September 1996) and 'Come rain or come shine' by Charlotte Packer, p96 (*The Independent* 15 February 1997); Ewan MacNaughton Associates on behalf of the Telegraph Group Limited for the article 'The grisly things that land on your plate' by Jenny Mc Cartney, p14 (*The Sunday Telegraph* 7 July 1996 © Telegraph Group Limited, 1996); MSI for an extract adapted from a restaurant review in 'The A List Review', p50 (*The Daily Mirror*, 22-28 May 1998); The National Magazine Company Limited for extracts from 'The agony and the ecstasy' by Anne Woodham, p36 and 'Desktop publishing' by Hilary Robinson p88 (*GoodHousekeeping*, June 1995); New Scientist for an extract from 'Day of the Sparrow' by Bob Holmes, pp16–18 (27 June 1998); News International Syndication for extracts from articles 'How grey matter can be red hot' by Anjana Ahuja, p58 (*The Times*, 16 October 1996 © Times Newspapers Limited, 1996); Octopus Books for an extract adapted from *Italian Cooking* by Anne Ager, p10; Penguin UK for an extract adapted from *Life's Other Secrets: The New Mathematics of the Living World* by Ian Stewart, p72 (Penguin Books, 1998 © Ian Stewart 1998); Philip Swindells for an extract adapted from 'Who's a pretty plant then', pp44–45 (*Welcome Aboard* Magazine, Jun/July 1998); Transworld Publishing Limited for an extract from *The Making of Memory* by Steven Rose, pp53–54.

Whilst every effort has been made to locate the owners of copyright, in some cases this has been unsuccessful. The publishers apologise for any omission of original sources and will be pleased to make the necessary arrangements at the first opportunity.

Printed and bound in Great Britain by Redwood Books, Trowbridge, Wiltshire

96 97 98 99 00 10 9 8 7 6 5 4 3 2 1

Contents

Introduction		iv
Unit 1	Sign of the Times	5
Unit 2	Call of the Wild	15
Unit 3	A Word in your Ear	25
Unit 4	A Fine Romance	35
Unit 5	All Right on the Night	44
Unit 6	Tip of my Tongue	53
Unit 7	A Matter of Taste	63
Unit 8	Go your own Way	72
Unit 9	Nose to the Grindstone	81
Unit 10	The Road Ahead	89
Answer key		97

Introduction

This workbook is designed to be used alongside the student's book and the exercises in each unit are generally based on the themes and topics found in the student's book.

Each unit in the workbook includes a wide variety of tasks and exercises, all designed to help you develop your vocabulary and practise the reading, writing and Use of English skills you need to pass the Cambridge Certificate of Proficiency in English examination (CPE). Even if you are not following a course based on the student's book, you will find the exercises useful.

As well as giving you practice in the exam-style tasks and exercises, this workbook also has a number of other important features:

- explanations of the main grammatical points with practice exercises
- interesting texts with either multiple-choice or comprehension questions
- practice of both composition and summary writing
- help with the correct use of punctuation in English
- help with pronunciation
- help with spelling
- vocabulary development
- practice in the use of idiomatic expressions and phrasal verbs

UNIT 1

Sign of the Times

VOCABULARY: Wordsearch

1 Find as many words as possible connected with the topic of hamburgers in the grid. Words may run horizontally or vertically. One has been done for you as an example.

```
T A K E A W A Y L A B C O W
Y O M N I P R E S E N T K L
H B (H A M B U R G E R) W H M
A J C U P R H V R X E M A E
R F R O Z E N R I T L G M A
D A S T R A W P L U I L B T
R S A E I C O N L N S O U L
O T H O L W I L L B H B R S
C F G R O U N D J U R A G E
K O A A K M C D O N A L D S
C O H E L E N B E E F I L A
A D S E A S O N I N G Z N M
F R I E S C C H A I N E R E
E H C O K E A M B L A N D E
```

2 Divide the words you have found into groups under these five headings:

Ingredients	Accessories	Opinions/Ideas	Places/Companies	Methods/Processes
_____	_____	_____	_____	_____
_____	_____	_____	_____	_____
_____	_____	_____	_____	_____
_____	_____	_____	_____	_____
	_____			

READING: Pre-reading task

1 Now think about another type of food – **pasta**. Think of as many words as you can which you associate with pasta and put them under the five headings. Do you need any other headings?

Ingredients	Accessories	Opinions/Ideas	Places/Companies	Processes/Methods
_____	_____	_____	_____	_____
_____	_____	_____	_____	_____
_____	_____	_____	_____	_____
_____	_____	_____	_____	_____

UNIT 1

2 Read this article about pasta quickly. How many of the words on your lists can you find in the article?

3 Read the text more carefully and answer the questions which follow.

Planet Pasta

Pasta, in one form or another, is a component of many cuisines around the world. Even where it is not part of the local cooking tradition, **it** is still generally available. All the more extraordinary, therefore, that sales of pasta in Britain should have increased 48% between 1991 and 1995, and continue to do so. A similar trend has been registered in France and the USA. Only the Italians, it seems, are consuming less of the stuff. So, what lies behind this trend?

First, let us consider pasta itself. Apart from putting a slab of meat on a fire, boiling an egg or eating vegetables raw, no dish in the world is much simpler than pasta. It consists of flour, egg and water. **It** is dropped into boiling water and requires no more skill in cooking than boiling an egg. Like an egg, it is appetizing or unappetizing according to the amount of time it is cooked, and like an egg there is some variation in the cooking time depending on whether you like it soft or prefer it to retain its resilience.

However, where other staples like rice or bread have survived and are eaten more or less as is, the almost unique characteristic of pasta is that it is no more than a savoury depository for other flavours: **those** of its innumerable sauces. No one you or I know eats pasta plain. At the very least, we add butter and the Chinese cook it in stock or add pungent spices.

This very combinatory capacity, of course, is one of the reasons for the ubiquity of pasta. Whatever your most prized and available flavours (fish, meat, fungi or vegetables), they can be combined with pasta, and this factor allowed it to migrate from its original Asian home to Italy, **whose** main foodstuff it has long been. It also permitted chefs around the world to experiment and invent means by which its flavour could be enhanced.

Pasta is also cheap, democratic, filling and nutritious. Its carbo-hydrates provide quickly convertible energy and whatever you add to it simply adds to its nutritional value. Finally, though there are some people who don't eat some of those additional ingredients, you would be hard put to find anyone who doesn't like it.

So, the question now is why pasta has found new favour in western culture in recent years. I would like to suggest a number of factors. The first and most important of **these** is the new democracy of the kitchen; the fact that neither meal-times nor the symbolic importance of the dinner table retain **their** former formality. Pasta is a rough-and-ready, quickly-prepared food fix. As it meets with universal favour and takes no great effort, it is available to all, and at any time. One cannot underestimate what this new ease of eating, at any time, under any circumstances means. **It** means freedom from planning because the ingredients are always available; it means quick and pungent satisfaction of appetite allied with facility; it is uncomplicated.

As the old habits of eating – as a family, with the usual cast of characters, with manners, table settings, etc. have died out under the exigencies of modern working hours and the absence of a woman stuck at home preparing food for husband and children, so pasta has advanced alongside, I might add, other quick fixes from the take-away to the stir fry, the pizza to the pre-washed salad. The influence **here** is American. It is Americans who invented the whole idea of the meal-on-the-move, the drive-in, the fast-food outlet, the franchised, standardized meal.

The next major influence is economic. When I was much younger, pasta was what one ate in restaurants: it was what one could afford, it was a known quantity, it seldom went wrong and wasn't pretentious, not requiring manners or formality of any kind. Pasta is user-friendly in much the same way as it is cook-friendly.

But if pasta has made great strides in the past few years, **it** has to be due to the emphasis placed on the 'healthy' Mediterranean diet. I can remember, many years ago, that when I reported in the British press that the Italian football team trained on pasta before a big match, I was thought scarcely believable. Pasta was considered a 'heavy' indigestible dish in Britain at that time. It was not long, however, before the sceptics realized that, in fact, we have few such excellent, short-term energy-providers as pasta. It is quickly absorbed, easily digested and gives instant results. In a world increasingly devoted to health and exercise, pasta was a natural.

I like to think, however, that the clinching argument in favour of pasta, and the reason why it is the fastest expanding food area in food marketing, is its accessibility. Pasta breaks down the distinction between cooking and eating: it brings out the inventive in even the rankest amateur, since almost anything can be thrown into a pasta sauce; it makes no demands on anyone. Even the most modest cook can produce miraculously good pasta – as it were, by accident. The democracy of pasta is based on the enjoyment factor. It is in fact a convivial dish, an always welcome dish, a leveller. If you combine that with the health factor, its accessibility to vegetarians and its low cost, the phenomenon becomes perfectly understandable.

Language work

1. What is it about pasta that the writer finds so surprising in paragraph one?

2. What essential quality of pasta is the focus of paragraph two?

3. Which word in paragraph three describes the group of foods to which pasta belongs?

4. In your own words, explain what the writer means by 'this combinatory capacity'. (line 32)

5. Which word in paragraph four is used to describe the fact that pasta is found everywhere?

6. What does the writer mean by the phrase which begins 'You would be hard put to find…'? (lines 47–48)

7. In your own words, explain what the writer means by the phrase 'the new democracy of the kitchen'. (line 54)

8. What two social changes are described as contributing to changes in eating habits in Western culture in recent years?

9. In your own words, explain why the writer chose to eat pasta in restaurants when he was younger.

10. Why were British people initially surprised to learn that Italian football players 'trained on pasta'? (line 92)

11. What does the writer mean by the phrase 'the clinching argument'? (lines 102–103)

UNIT 1

Summary

1. Use the article to make a list of the main reasons why pasta has become so popular in Western countries.
2. Put the list of points in order, from the least to the most important according to what the writer has told us.
3. Write a paragraph explaining these reasons, beginning with the sentence below. Try to use some of the words and phrases in the box to help you structure your paragraph. Use your own words as far as you can.

> firstly   secondly   thirdly   finally   furthermore   therefore
> lastly   what's more   moreover   in addition   likewise

There are a number of reasons why pasta has become such a popular food in Western countries like Britain in recent years...

Reference skills

Look back at these words which are in **bold** in the text. In each case say what the word is referring to. One has been done for you as an example.

0	it (line 4)	=	*pasta*
1	it (line 16)	=	
2	those (line 28)	=	
3	whose (line 38)	=	
4	these (line 53)	=	
5	their (line 56)	=	
6	it (line 62)	=	
7	here (line 76)	=	
8	it (line 88)	=	

Dependent prepositions

Put one of the prepositions from the box into each of these phrases from the article without looking at the text. When you have finished the exercise, look back to check your answers.

> to   from   of   into   with

1. Apart _____ putting a slab of meat on a fire... (line 13)
2. It consists _____ flour, eggs and water. (lines 15–16)
3. Your most prized and available flavours can be combined _____ pasta... (lines 34–35)
4. As it meets _____ universal favour... (lines 58–59)
5. It means freedom _____ planning... (lines 62–63)
6. In a world increasingly devoted _____ health and exercise... (lines 99–101)
7. Almost anything can be thrown _____ a pasta sauce... (lines 108–109)
8. Its accessibility _____ vegetarians... (lines 115–116)

Vocabulary

Can you add any more words from the article to the lists you wrote before reading the text?

8

GRAMMAR: Causatives

Remember the use and form of the causative *have/get*:

Form: | subject + *to have/to get* + object of the verb + past participle of main verb |

      I   am having   my car   serviced.

N.B. This form exists in a variety of tenses and in each case it is the verb *to have* or *to get* which indicates the tense.

Use: mainly to talk about professional services to a customer:
   I'm having my car repaired. (This means that someone is repairing my car for me.)

compare with:
   I'm repairing my car. (This means that I'm doing it myself.)

Finish each of the following sentences so that it **as similar as possible in meaning to the sentence printed before it,** but uses the causative form.

   Example: My car needs servicing.
   Answer: It's time I <u>had/got my car serviced</u>.

1. Somebody needs to translate this document into English for us.
   We need to _____
2. They will shorten trousers for you at the cleaners.
   You can _____
3. Your central heating boiler should have an annual service.
   You should _____
4. I shall ask a professional photographer to take my passport photo.
   I shall _____
5. We will employ a catering company to prepare the food for the party.
   We'll _____
6. It's not necessary to find an engineer; you can repair it yourself.
   You don't have _____
7. Someone is making a new set of dining-room curtains for us.
   We _____
8. It was a mistake to let a gardener paint the outside of our house.
   We shouldn't _____
9. Louisa has been cutting my hair for years.
   I've _____
10. Ask Tom Smith if you want someone to cut down those trees.
    If you want _____
11. I remember having to go to the dentist's for a filling.
    I remember having _____
12. It would have been possible for them to deliver your new sofa on Monday.
    You _____

UNIT 1

HELP WITH PUNCTUATION 1: Full stops and capital letters

There is a tendency in English to use a large number of short sentences. In contrast to some other languages, simplicity in sentence structure is regarded as good style in English writing.

The full stop (.) is, therefore, a very common punctuation mark. Whereas commas (,) are used to show the parts of a sentence, and to clarify meaning, the full stop is used to indicate that a sentence has come to an end. It is followed by a capital letter.

Capital letters are also used for:
- proper names and their adjectives: *England, English, John, Londoner*
- days and months; *Monday, January*
- companies, organizations, clubs, etc.: *Manchester United, British Airways*
- geographical names: *the North Pole, the West End of London*
- for the pronoun *I*

In this passage there are no full stops, commas or capital letters. First read the text to get an idea of its content, then decide where the sentences should begin and end, and add the required punctuation.

> as any italian housewife will tell you homemade pasta is not difficult to make it does however require patience and time which is why i tend to make it on sunday mornings people who have a gift for making pastry or bread will have very little problem in making pasta as many of the skills applied to all three are the same the most important thing to remember is that you need plenty of uncluttered work surface a very large chopping board or marble slab is ideal but modern laminate worktops are quite adequate an extra large rolling pin will make the rolling of the pasta dough much easier if you plan to go into pasta making in a big way then it may be worth your while to buy a pasta machine at the turn of a handle this will give you many different shapes and thicknesses of pasta these machines manufactured in northern italy are now widely available in specialist kitchenware shops all over the world

PHRASAL VERBS: Phrasal verbs with *out*

In the box are some verbs in the infinitive. Choose one verb from the box to complete the phrasal verb in each of the sentences **1–10** and write the correct form of the verb in the space. One has been done for you as an example.

| bring   call   come   draw   get   ~~go~~   hold   fall   pull   sell   watch |

0   Darren said that certain types of trainer had _gone_ completely out of fashion.
1   One supermarket has _____ out in favour of banning cigarette sales.
2   Another supermarket is _____ out a book on healthy eating in December.
3   Tony's very shy. Get chatting to him and see if you can _____ him out a bit.
4   Justin and Rachel are not talking, They have _____ out with each other.
5   Tracy said she'd _____ a lot out of that course in media studies.
6   No agreement was reached. The strikers decided to _____ out for a better deal.
7   The supermarket has completely _____ out of cheap washing powder.
8   As you go round the flea market _____ out for pickpockets as well as bargains.
9   The doctor can't see you at the moment, he's been _____ out on an emergency.
10 Tim was _____ out of a parking place when the accident happened.

UNIT 1

WRITING: Linking words and phrases

Read this article written by an anti-smoking campaigner. The linking words and phrases have been taken out. Choose the best word or phrase **A**, **B**, **C** or **D** to fill each gap, **1–12**. One has been done for you as an example.

Smoking is known to be one of the greatest single causes of death in our society. Too little seems to be done, (**0**) _C_ , to stop young people taking up the habit in the first place.

(**1**) _____, cigarettes are openly on sale in many public places and laws governing the minimum age at which they can be bought often seem to be ignored. (**2**) _____, cigarette advertising continues to figure largely in some parts of the media, (**3**) _____ recent moves to outlaw this, and is, (**4**) _____, often targeted at young people.

(**5**) _____ anti-smoking campaigns have been organized in recent years, these seem not to have been particularly effective, (**6**) _____ the rise in the numbers of young people, especially girls, who take up smoking each year. (**7**) _____ supporting such campaigns in principle, I would like to propose an alternative approach.

(**8**) _____, I think that the advertising of cigarettes should be completely banned from all aspects of the media. (**9**) _____, the sale of cigarettes should be more tightly controlled to ensure that the law regarding underage smokers is respected. And, (**10**) _____, cigarettes should not be sold in places such as cafés and supermarkets frequented by young people and families. Their sale should (**11**) _____ be restricted to licensed tobacconists and sharp penalties should be imposed on those breaking the law, particularly those selling cigarettes on the black market.

(**12**) _____, I would like to add that, of course, it is the duty of parents, teachers and other responsible adults to set a good example; by not smoking!

0	**A** Although	**B** Despite	**C** However	**D** Moreover
1	**A** Likewise	**B** To begin with	**C** Whilst	**D** Therefore
2	**A** however	**B** moreover	**C** nonetheless	**D** though
3	**A** otherwise	**B** thanks to	**C** despite	**D** however
4	**A** what's more	**B** likewise	**C** therefore	**D** even though
5	**A** Despite	**B** However	**C** Furthermore	**D** Although
6	**A** resulting	**B** especially	**C** instead	**D** given
7	**A** However	**B** Whilst	**C** Finally	**D** Therefore
8	**A** Although	**B** Whilst	**C** Firstly	**D** Especially
9	**A** Furthermore	**B** Therefore	**C** Instead	**D** Otherwise
10	**A** to sum up	**B** secondly	**C** in addition	**D** in spite of this
11	**A** however	**B** nonetheless	**C** instead	**D** likewise
12	**A** In addition	**B** Consequently	**C** Therefore	**D** Finally

HELP WITH SPELLING 1

Spelling in English is sometimes difficult as there is no direct relationship between the sounds and the letters used to represent them. Also, the 'rules' of spelling are complicated and it is not useful to try and learn them. You have to do what English speakers learn to do – remember the spelling of each new word as you come across it.

There are, however, some tips which might help you to improve your spelling in English and these can be useful to remember. But don't forget, there will always be some exceptions to even the simplest general rules.

UNIT 1

The silent e

Many words end in the letter *e*, but in a number of words this *e* is silent, or unpronounced:
   care /keə/   believe /bɪli:v/   achieve /ətʃi:v/   definite /defɪnɪt/   nice /naɪs/

Compare these words which end with a sounded letter e:
   see /si:/   agree /əgri:/

When adding a suffix beginning with a vowel (**-i**ng, - **a**ble, **-e**st) to a word ending in a silent *e*, then the letter *e* is usually dropped:
   care → caring→   believe → believable   nice → nicest

When adding a suffix beginning with a consonant (e.g. - **l**y, **-m**ent, **-f**ul) to a word ending in a silent *e*, then the letter *e* is usually retained:
   achieve → achievement   definite → definitely   care → careful

The main exceptions are words ending in *c* and *g* sounds. So, try to remember:

noti**ce**	→	noti**ci**ng	→	noti**cea**ble
chan**ge**	→	chan**gi**ng	→	chan**gea**ble
mana**ge**	→	mana**gi**ng	→	mana**gea**ble

Complete each of the spaces in this passage by adding a suffix to the word in the column on the right-hand side. The word you write should make sense in the context of the passage.

John got up, looked out of the window and (**1**) _____ started	IMMEDIATE
(**2**) _____. After five days of pouring rain and wet clothes, he	SMILE
saw to his (**3**) _____ that the sun had come out. He had	AMAZE
always known the weather in Scotland would be (**4**) _____ ,	CHANGE
but he wasn't prepared for the pleasant surprise of (**5**) _____	SEE
the sun (**6**) _____ down on him this particular morning. He	SHINE
could (**7**) _____ believe his luck.	BARE
For, according to the (**8**) _____ he had come to with the	AGREE
(**9**) _____ of the hotel, this was the day when he would go	MANAGE
sailing round the (**10**) _____ Isle of Skye, which all his friends	LOVE
had told him was (**11**) _____ worth doing.	DEFINITE

GRAMMAR: Review of past tenses

Remember the form and use of the past tenses:

Present Perfect:

Form: | *have* + the past participle of the verb |

Uses:
- to talk about past experiences in your life:
  I've been to Egypt three times.

- to talk about things which have happened in unfinished periods of time:
  I've drunk too much coffee today.
  I've learnt how to use a PC.

- the present perfect continuous to talk about things which started in the past and are still happening now:
  I've been painting my room since this morning. I should be finshed by tonight.

- to talk about things which have happened recently:
  She's **just written** a letter to him.

Present Perfect vs Past Simple:

If you need to decide which tense to use, ask yourself the question *When?*
I've never been to Italy, but I *went* to Greece last summer.

I've never been to Italy.
When? In my life – the exact time is not important so we use the present perfect.

I went to Greece last summer.
When? Last summer – the time is important so we use the past simple.

The past simple is used to talk about things which happened in finished periods of time.

Past Perfect:

Form: | *had* + past participle of the verb |

Use:
When we tell a story, we set a time in the past in which the narrative takes place. When we refer to actions and periods before that, the Past Perfect is used:

*When we got back to the house, he **had removed** all the furniture.*
(First he removed the furniture and then we got back. Past perfect.)

*When we got back to the house, he **removed** all the furniture.*
(First we got back and then we removed the furniture. Past simple.)

*I **had been living** in Greece for five years when I decided to buy a car.*
(The past perfect continuous is used to talk about events which began in the past and which continued up until another action in the past.)

Put the verbs in brackets in this text into the correct tense according to the context. The verbs may be either simple or continuous forms of the **past**, the **present perfect** or the **past perfect** tenses. One has been done for you as an example.

Many children start going for dental checkups at an early age, but Kelly Smithers was fourteen years old when she (**0**) __went__ (go) for the first time. It (**1**) _____ (be) not a happy experience.

Until then Kelly (**2**) _____ (be) lucky. She (**3**) _____ (always have) good teeth and (**4**) _____ (never have) suffered from toothache. But for two or three months Kelly (**5**) _____ (get) pain, on and off, in one of her teeth. So, her mother (**6**) _____ (decide) that a trip to the dentist (**7**) _____ (be) necessary.

It (**8**) _____ (turn) out to be a terrible experience for Kelly. She (**9**) _____ (have) twelve fillings in one sitting and (**10**) _____ (be) in great pain. Since then, Kelly (**11**) _____ (suffer) from dental phobia and (**12**) _____ (never have) the courage to go to the dentist's again.

But then, three months ago, Kelly (**13**) _____ (sign) up for a session at *Feelgood Dentistry*. She (**14**) _____ (start) to have toothache again and (**15**) _____ (realize) that she (**16**) _____ (need) to do something about it. At *Feelgood* she (**17**) _____ (have) regular counselling sessions and (**18**) _____ (be) given the chance to talk through her problems thoroughly. 'It (**19**) _____ (be) wonderful so far,' she says, 'I (**20**) _____ (begin) to understand what lies behind my phobia and so I should be able to overcome it soon.'

UNIT 1

USE OF ENGLISH: Cloze passage

Put **one** word from the box into each of the spaces in the text. One has been done for you as an example.

| with | against | during | in | of | ~~just~~ | out | to | up | created | sending |
| came | take | try | been | way | contents | times | who | what | the |

The Grisly Things that Land on your Plate

Imagine finding a sheep's tooth in a packet of peanuts, a dead spider in your frozen pizza or broken glass in a bread roll. These are (**0**) _just_ a few of the items that found their (**1**) _____ on to consumers' tables last year, according (**2**) _____ a report on consumer complaints by Alan Richards.

His job is to (**3**) _____ to identify when and how the objects got into the product. About ten percent of claims turn (**4**) _____ to be unfounded. Tests on wasps and flies in pots of jam, for example, often show they were not cooked along (**5**) _____ the product in a factory, but fell (**6**) _____ much later – unnoticed by the outraged consumer, (**7**) _____ instantly blamed the producer.

But, products often end (**8**) _____ back at the factory for investigations into (**9**) _____ went wrong. In the past, screws and metal rivets have fallen from machines (**10**) _____ processing, or lightbulbs have shattered, (**11**) _____ shards of glass into the product. But these days, most factories (**12**) _____ great care to ensure that their quality systems are very thorough indeed.

Factory workers have (**13**) _____ known to sabotage food because they had a grudge (**14**) _____ the management. This is the only explanation for how one consumer (**15**) _____ to buy a carton of milk which contained the entire (**16**) _____ of a fly-trap – over one hundred insects.

Occasionally, problems are (**17**) _____ by mistakenly high levels of chemicals in food. Last year, Mr Richards tested a can of custard that stank (**18**) _____ disinfectant. A chemical found in artificial food flavouring was (**19**) _____ culprit – it had been added at a strength fifty (**20**) _____ the normal level.

Vocabulary

Find these words in the passage. One has been done for you as an example.

0 a noun meaning *people who buy* — _consumers_
1 an adjective meaning *not based on fact* — _____
2 an adjective meaning *very angry* — _____
3 a verb meaning *broken into small pieces* — _____
4 a noun meaning *small, sharp pieces* — _____
5 a verb meaning *deliberately damage/spoil something* — _____
6 a noun meaning *a wish to get revenge on someone* — _____
7 a noun meaning *smelled badly* — _____
8 a noun meaning *the person or thing responsible for something bad* — _____

Summary

Using your own words, write a paragraph of about **50 words** explaining the various reasons why strange objects sometimes turn up in food.

UNIT 2

Call of the Wild

VOCABULARY: Wordsearch

1 Find the names of as many animals as possible in the grid. Words may run horizontally or vertically. One has been done for you as an example.

```
P Y T H O N  P P F R O G B Q
U O A U B I R D S N A K E L
P A R R O T H L C A T I E R
P W A G A V O M O U S E P A
Y K N F O X R A R A B B I T
B A T I A Z S M P N K U G L
G N U S F E E W I D U C K A
O W L H R D O D O O X H C B
O R A N G U T A N G J I H R
W J W Q F L Y T O K A P I A
H S H E E P O H M L G M C D
A W D A C H S H U N D U K O
L A M B A I B U L L N N E R
E W A S P N M D E E R K N M
```

2 Divide the animals that you have found into these categories:

Mammals	Birds	Amphibians/Reptiles	Insects	Others

3 Add the names of any other animals you know to your lists.

UNIT 2

4 Match each adjective on the left with an animal on the right to make a common simile. One has been done for you as an example. Are these animals associated with the same adjectives or qualities in your language?

dead	parrot	*As dead as a dodo.*
blind	dodo	
busy	peacock	
free	ox	
sick	owl	
proud	mule	
quiet	mouse	
sly	fox	
strong	bird	
stubborn	bee	
wise	bat	

READING

Read the text carefully and for questions 1–5, choose the best alternative A, B, C or D which fits best.

Day of the sparrow

Isolation has profound effects. It can pull a group of people together or drive the individual over the brink. In the natural world, **it** helps create new species of plants and animals. Indeed, without physical barriers, the sea, mountains, deserts, etc., to separate organisms, the Earth would probably have only half of its present number of species.

So, for a botanist like Wendy Strahm, a visit to a new island should be full of encounters with surprising plants that have evolved in isolation from the rest of the world. But **it** is usually more like just another day at the office. 'It's depressing. I go to any island and I already know the flora,' says Wendy, who has clocked up years of fieldwork on the tropical isles of the Indian Ocean. 'The same trees have been planted and the same plants have been introduced from elsewhere. We're turning the world into something identical everywhere.' Plants such as lantana and strawberry guava and animals like rats, sparrows and cats, are steadily invading the Earth's ecosystems and ousting the natural inhabitants.

Slowly, conservation biologists and ecologists are realizing that this homogenization of the world's species is as big a threat as global warming, desertification and deforestation – and just as deserving of policy makers' attention. Much of the impact of global warming, for example, could in time be reversed, but once you homogenize the biodiversity of the world, there's really no turning back.

Even today, relatively few biologists, and still fewer non-scientists, have any inkling of the scale of the problem. Even those studying alien species tend to get engrossed in trying to understand and manage local populations rather than considering the broader picture. It's very easy for someone to see what is happening around them, but it's not easy to see over the horizon – that **this** is just a local example of something that's happening all over.

Oceanic islands such as New Zealand and Mauritius have sustained the worse ecological damage from invading species so far, but continental areas have not escaped unscathed. Nearly two thousand species of introduced plants have become naturalized in Australia, for example, and between two and four thousand, depending on who you ask, infest the United States. Whilst in Britain, forty-three percent of wild plant species have come from elsewhere. What's more, the rate of species introductions appears to be increasing. The main reason for **this** is the boom in international trade which brings more ships and more accidental stowaways from a wider range of foreign ports into an area.

But sheer numbers of exotic species don't

mean much. We need to distinguish between catastrophic invaders and minor annoyances, according to Howard Mooney, an ecologist at Stanford University. As a general rule of thumb, many ecologists reckon that about ten percent of species introduced actually 'take' and establish naturalized populations, and about ten percent of **these** become a nuisance. But predicting which ten percent has proved to be a challenge.

One hallmark of a problem invader is that it often creates an ecological role for itself that did not exist before in the ecosystem it has infiltrated. A good example is the devastation that rats, cats and pigs have caused to ground nesting birds on islands with no native land-based predators. And on Hawaii, a type of Africa grass produces much more dead foliage than native grasses, **causing** more frequent and widespread fires that drive out native plants.

The best way – indeed the only practical way – to combat the threat of introduced species is to keep them out in the first place. Ideally, countries would simply block the movement of species likely to create problems. But to do **that** scientists need a better understanding of which these species are. Mooney has just launched a three-year programme to try to predict problem species more accurately and develop better ways of keeping **them** in check.

But if a potentially dangerous species does take hold in a new country, the priority should be to eradicate it before the trouble starts. 'So many of these invasive problems have not been nipped in the bud,' says Wendy Stahm. So far, this call for preventative action has caused barely a ripple in most policy makers' ponds. With a few exceptions, notably New Zealand, funding is miserly as the global-trade juggernaut rolls on.

Comprehension

1. Why does Wendy Stahm feel depressed when she visits a new island?
   A She finds nothing new there.
   B She's already visited so many islands.
   C The new plants she finds no longer surprise her.
   D She finds only a predictable selection of plants.

2. Why is homogenization of species more of a threat than global warming?
   A It's happening more quickly.
   B It will affect more species.
   C Nothing is being done about it.
   D Its effects may be longer-lasting.

3. According to the article, what may scientists have failed to realize about the homogenization of species?
   A The real cause of the problem.
   B Where the problem is at its worst.
   C The extent of the problem.
   D Its effect on their local areas.

4. In a given area, scientists have found it difficult to predict how many new species
   A may be introduced.
   B will become established.
   C would cause a problem.
   D could be accommodated.

5. What does Wendy Stahm see as the best way to deal with individual problems?
   A A speedy initial response.
   B Research into movement of species.
   C Prediction of where problems will occur.
   D Action against all introduced species.

UNIT 2

Vocabulary

Look back at the text and find words or phrases that mean the following. Paragraph numbers are given in brackets and one has been done for you as an example.

- **0** a phrasal verb meaning *to use an amount of time* (2) — *clocked up*
- **1** a verb meaning *to remove or replace by force* (2) — _____
- **2** a phrase meaning *eventually* (3) — _____
- **3** a noun meaning *a vague idea* (4) — _____
- **4** an adjective meaning *not affected* (5) — _____
- **5** a noun meaning *a large increase* (5) — _____
- **6** a noun meaning *unofficial/illegal passengers* (5) — _____
- **7** a noun meaning *things which irritate* (6) — _____
- **8** a noun meaning *a distinguishing feature* (7) — _____
- **9** a noun meaning *green plant material* (7) — _____
- **10** a phrasal verb meaning *to remove or replace by force* (7) — _____
- **11** a verb meaning *control* (8) — _____
- **12** an idiomatic expression meaning *stopped at the very beginning* (9) — _____
- **13** a noun meaning *a large overpowering force* (9) — _____

Reference skills

Look back at these words which are in **bold** in the text. In each case say what the word is referring to. One has been done for you as an example.

- **0** it (line 3) = *isolation*
- **1** it (line 12) = _____
- **2** this (line 40) = _____
- **3** this (line 54) = _____
- **4** these (line 66) = _____
- **5** causing (line 75) = _____
- **6** that (line 82) = _____
- **7** them (line 87) = _____

Summary

Using your own words as far as possible, write a paragraph of about **50 words** on the subject of introduced species. In your paragraph explain:

- what introduced species are
- why introduced species cause problems
- what can be done to deal with such problems

UNIT 2

Word families and wordstress

1 Complete the grid with the missing words from these families and mark each of the words to show the wordstress. The first word family has been completed for you as an example.

	verb	noun	adjective
0	sur<u>prise</u>	*sur<u>prise</u>*	*sur<u>pris</u>ing*
1	depress	_____	_____
2	_____	globe	_____
3	_____	_____	invading/invasive
4	_____	prevention	_____

5 What is the difference between *invading* and *invasive*?
_____

6 Which other word in the table has two adjectives? What does each mean?
_____

2 Mark the wordstress on these nouns.
What is the adjective formed from each of the nouns?
Is the wordstress in the same place in the adjective?

	noun	adjective
1	ecology	_____
2	catastrophe	_____
3	continent	_____
4	photograph	_____
5	biology	_____

3 Mark the wordstress on these verbs.
What is the noun formed from each of the verbs?
Is the wordstress in the same place in the noun?

	verb	noun
1	homogenize	_____
2	populate	_____
3	devastate	_____
4	isolate	_____
5	naturalize	_____
6	infiltrate	_____
7	punctuate	_____
8	pronounce	_____

GRAMMAR: Relative pronouns

Remember: *the person who…*   *the thing which…*
           the place which (I like)… *the place where (something happened)…*

1 Complete each of the sentences **1–6** by using a relative pronoun to make a sentence in the context of the passage on introduced species. One has been done for you as an example.

0 A botanist *is a person who studies plants.*
1 Sparrows _____
2 Wendy Stahm _____
3 Lantana _____
4 Howard Mooney _____
5 New Zealand _____
6 African grasses _____

19

UNIT 2

2 Join these sentences together using an appropriate relative pronoun. Can the relative pronoun be omitted in any of these sentences? One has been done for you as an example.

0 I met a lady. She was very keen on dogs.
   I met a lady who was very keen on dogs. (relative pronoun cannot be omitted)

1 I saw a parrot in a shop. It was exactly the type I wanted.

2 We had some prawns for lunch. They must have been off.

3 There was a popular soap-opera in the Far East. It starred an orang-utan.

4 Many whales turn up on beaches. On these beaches there are no people.

5 I knocked on the door. It looked like the right one.

6 I wanted to make a film. I wanted the film to highlight the problems of dolphins.

7 John Small is the man's name. He sold me the tarantula.

8 A spider has escaped from the zoo. It is thought to be very dangerous.

9 *Bleak House* is a novel by Dickens. It's probably the best one he ever wrote.

10 People are invited to join the organization. They should be interested in animal welfare.

11 A new pet shop has just opened. You can buy snakes there.

12 The orang-utan could play the piano. I never thought I'd see such a thing.

GRAMMAR: Use of the article

In this text from the student's book, the articles have been taken out. In each space write one of the following:
  – the definite article *the*
  – the indefinite article *a/an*
  – no article (–)

When you have completed the exercise, look back at page 36 of the student's book to check.

If somebody finds, say, (**1**) _____ rabbit that's been run over and has (**2**) _____ broken leg, (**3**) _____ last thing one should do is take it to (**4**) _____ vet and waste (**5**) _____ money on trying to pin it together and then put it in (**6**) _____ cage. (**7**) _____ kindest thing to do is knock it on (**8**) _____ head. Now that would horrify (**9**) _____ average town dweller, but what we're trying to do is preserve (**10**) _____ genuine rural habitats. I'm afraid the trouble is, and it may seem unkind to say it in this way, but (**11**) _____ certain people are merely over-sentimental about _____ (**12**) animals, and it really tells you more about (**13**) _____ people concerned than it does about (**14**) _____ well-being of wildlife.

HELP WITH SPELLING 2: Double consonants

- When a suffix is added to a word, especially a suffix beginning with a vowel, the consonant is often doubled.
  This happens in words of one syllable where a single final consonant follows a single vowel:
  set → se**tt**ing
  hot → ho**tt**er
  knit → kni**tt**ed

- It doesn't happen where words already have two consonants or two vowels together:
  sta**rt** → started
  m**ee**t → meeting

- In two-syllable or longer words the stress is important. Where the stress falls on the final syllable, then single final consonants are doubled:
  for<u>get</u> → forgetting   compare with: <u>bene</u>fit → benefited
  ad<u>mit</u> → admittedly   <u>open</u> → opening
  re<u>fer</u> → referred   <u>market</u> → marketing

- Be careful in words where the stress changes when suffixes are added:
  pre<u>fer</u> → pre<u>ferr</u>ed → <u>prefer</u>ence

- Words that end with silent *e* do not need double consonants when the *e* is dropped:
  care → caring

- Remember these exceptions:
  write → writing → written   develop → developing → developed

Complete each of the spaces in this passage by adding a suffix to the word in the column on the right-hand side. The word you write should make sense in the context of the passage.

Suzy Stokes works for the (**1**) _____ department of a large	MARKET
company which makes (**2**) _____ garments. It was Suzy who	KNIT
introduced the idea of (**3**) _____ dog hair to the company,	SPIN
and she has been responsible for (**4**) _____ the technology	DEVELOP
needed to produce yarns for the material.	
At the (**5**) _____, many people doubted that the idea would	BEGIN
take off, and only Suzy's (**6**) _____ approach prevented the	COMMIT
whole project from being (**7**) _____.	DROP
'It really hadn't (**8**) _____ to people that there could be a	OCCUR
market for the materials,' Suzy remembers, 'and (**9**) _____	TRANSFER
resources from other projects was not really (**10**) _____.'	PERMIT
But Suzy's determination paid off: at a recent sales (**11**) _____,	CONFER
dog-hair products were hailed as the company's largest growth area.	

UNIT 2

GRAMMAR: Expressing cause and result

For each of the sentences, write a new sentence **as similar as possible in meaning to the original sentence**, but using the word given. This word **must not be altered** in any way.

1 Whale strandings are often the result of illness or injury.
cause

_____

2 The introduction of African grasses led to more frequent fires.
resulted

_____

3 The result of isolation has often been the creation of new species.
leads

_____

4 Pollution may be responsible for the dolphins' loss of immunity to the virus.
blame

_____

5 Mass strandings are often caused by disorientation.
result

_____

6 Pollution is not always the culprit in environmental disasters.
blamed

_____

7 A TV programme is to blame for the latest fashion for exotic pets.
led

_____

8 Hunting is thought to have resulted in the extinction of the dodo.
cause

_____

PHRASAL VERBS: Phrasal verbs with *up* and *down*

Write **one** word in each of the spaces to complete the phrasal verb.

1 The botanist's theory has been _____ up by newly-discovered evidence.
2 After his accident, Jed didn't _____ up to going to the party.
3 After three weeks holiday, I had a lot of work to _____ up with.
4 I'm sorry to _____ this up, but I've found a misprint in this contract.
5 I can't get this zip to _____ up, it must be broken.
6 The contract for the new project will be _____ up next week.
7 The completion of the new by-pass will be _____ up due to a strike by construction workers.
8 I'm afraid there's no truth in the story, Geoff _____ it up as a joke.
9 He _____ up a lot of debts in the town and then disappeared without a trace.
10 A new organization is being _____ up for those concerned about the welfare of dolphins.

HELP WITH PUNCTUATION 2: Commas

The comma is used:

- after the salutation and close in letters:
  Dear Sir,
  Yours sincerely,

- in lists:
  The comma is used with words, phrases and clauses.
  Choose the best answer A, B, C or D.

- to mark out adverbs and clauses:
  Recently, there has been a change of attitude.
  As I had already seen the film, I found the visit to the cinema rather boring.

- when two clauses are joined by a conjunction:
  I hoped to catch up with Mary at the station, but she was too quick for me.

- to show that an idea is in parenthesis:
  The whole expedition was, I'm sorry to say, a complete waste of time.

- to prevent misreading:
  The girl ran around the room ten minutes after she fell asleep. (ambiguous)
  The girl ran around the room, ten minutes after she fell asleep. (clear)

In this letter there are no commas. Put commas in where they are needed.

---

27 Acacia Avenue
Harmborough
Surrey

The Manager
Pet city
Manchester

Dear sir

Recently I read an article which said that Pet City was the best place to buy tarantulas. As I would like to buy one as a pet I am writing to ask if you have any in stock at the moment.

Unfortunately I have never had a pet spider before so I was wondering if you could send me some information about the best way to look after them. For example are your tarantulas sold with cages and bedding or do I have to pay for these separately? I already have a pet dog and a small python but no other spiders. Do you think my tarantula will be lonely? Should I buy two or will that lead to other problems?

I would be grateful to receive the answer to these questions together with your pricelist a brochure any other information you may have about tarantulas and details of how to get to your shop from the city centre.

Yours faithfully
A Strangelove

UNIT 2

VOCABULARY: Idiomatic uses of animal vocabulary

Use **one** of the animal names in the box as a verb to complete each of the sentences. One has been done for you as an example.

> dog   worm   badger   fox   fish   ~~wolf~~

0 The way David __wolfed__ down the sandwich you'd think he hadn't eaten for a week.
1 Derek has been _____ by misfortune all his life.
2 Amy _____ her mother to buy her some sweets.
3 The police were completely _____ by the mystery of the missing manuscript.
4 When Sally said her dress was nothing special, she was really _____ for complements.
5 Trevor is very secretive, it's difficult trying to _____ information out of him.

FORMAL AND INFORMAL LANGUAGE

Choose the best word or phrase from the alternatives in italics to complete this semi-formal letter in an appropriate style.

Cycling Holidays Ltd.
York YO13 AR2
23 February

24 Oaklands Avenue
London
NE5 RE4

Dear Sir,

I am (**1**) *writing/dropping you a line* to ask for (**2**) *more/further* information about the cycling holidays you (**3**) *put on/organize* in the Yorkshire Dales.

I (**4**) *noticed/spotted* your (**5**) *advert/advertisement* in the Yorkshire Tourist magazine and I was pleasantly (**6**) *surprised/taken aback* to see (**7**) *the wide range/all the different types* of holiday you have (**8**) *for the taking/on offer*. I (**9**) *feel sure/wouldn't mind betting* that one of your holidays will (**10**) *be exactly what I am looking for/suit me down to the ground*.

I would be (**11**) *grateful/chuffed*, therefore, (**12**) *to get/to receive* a copy of your (**13**) *latest/newest* brochure, (**14**) *together with/and don't forget* a booking form and price list.

Looking forward to (**15**) *having your reply/hearing from you*.

Yours (**16**) *sincerely/faithfully*,
A. Reader

Writing: a formal letter

Imagine you work at Cycling Holidays Ltd. Write a reply of about 150 words to the letter above. You should:
  – use an appropriate formal letter layout
  – thank the customer for their letter and enquiry
  – give information about availability, special offers, latest booking date, etc.

UNIT 3

A Word in your Ear

IDIOMATIC EXPRESSIONS

In this section, you must choose the word, **A**, **B**, **C** or **D** which best completes each sentence.

1. John Archer's book is selling like hot _____.
   A stuff **B** cakes **C** property **D** soup
2. In any profession, you have to learn to take the _____ with the smooth.
   A hard **B** stodgy **C** rough **D** coarse
3. Some people take a _____ view of commercial fiction.
   A dim **B** low **C** poor **D** dull
4. The new secretary seems a bit lazy, she doesn't really _____ her weight.
   A push **B** give **C** act **D** pull
5. I'm sorry I missed the appointment, it must have _____ my mind.
   A missed **B** left **C** slipped **D** dropped
6. A bad management decision _____ disaster for the company.
   A drew **B** spelt **C** lay **D** sprang
7. David took great _____ to make sure his spelling was accurate.
   A troubles **B** efforts **C** trials **D** pains
8. It took Anna a long time to get the _____ of the new computer programme.
   A hang **B** grips **C** means **D** grasp
9. Tony _____ exception to Rachel's comments about his dress sense.
   A found **B** took **C** made **D** gave
10. Danny found it hard to _____ any headway with his German homework.
    A get **B** make **C** do **D** set

READING

Read the article and then answer the questions which follow.

Mind your language

Bill Saunders on the need to communicate internationally at all levels of business.

Business is becoming more international and secretaries will increasingly need international communication skills. Secretaries do not necessarily need to travel or work for an organization involved in international trade to encounter clients or even colleagues with whom English, although not **their** first language, is the only means of communication.

25

In the UK, ironically, despite the fact that the country is becoming more popular as a location for international business, the reputation of the local workforce for linguistic expertise is plummeting. This year at The London Secretary Show, two seminars will be held with the aim of proving that communication across language and cultural barriers is easier than many British people imagine.

As Anne Hamilton of the language consultants *Rendezvous*, who will be conducting a seminar on coping on the telephone in French, German and Spanish, says there is no knowing when **such skills** might become necessary. Even if a secretary currently never has to deal with clients who do not speak English, it may be necessary in the future. And a secretary is often the first point of contact between the company and the outside world. It is quite possible that, as such, secretaries may well find themselves liaising between the English-speaking world and a non-English speaking company.

Hamilton recognizes that the telephone is an intimidating instrument on which to conduct a conversation in a foreign language. Indeed, some people are not entirely happy with **it** in their mother tongue. But its very immediacy makes it a useful tool for developing language skills. *Rendezvous* offers courses in language tuition conducted entirely over the phone. Hamilton does not believe that someone has to be fluent in order to communicate in a foreign language by telephone, or even have any serious grounding in the language at all.

Rendezvous specializes in training in languages for specific purposes. **Its** clients include staff at ports and airports who have to issue simple instructions or directions in more than one language. Staff are trained to cope with the limited phrases they will need by acting out scenarios.

The **same methods** can be applied to secretaries. Hamilton says nobody necessarily expects a secretary to 'pass the time of day with them'. It is enough to be able to identify which language is being spoken and to give some sign to the caller that they will be passed on to someone who can deal with the call. A simple 'Hang on' in the given language will convey that the call is not a dialogue of the deaf. **Such an approach** also requires no knowledge of irregular verbs or complicated tenses. Even a handful of **such phrases** can increase confidence and make the experience of handling a foreign language call 'exhilarating rather than intimidating'.

Helen Vandeville of *Flagship Language Strategies* also believes that some knowledge is better than none. 'It is much easier to learn a language superficially,' she says. Secretaries should acquire language skills, if only to be able to offer basic hospitality, such as asking a visitor to sit down. Vandeville has written and published a series of guides on the business use of a number of languages.

At The London Secretary Show, *Flagship* will be conducting a seminar in global communication skills, covering not only language, but also sensibility to other cultures. The business cultures of some countries offer more potential pitfalls than others. Body language can send the wrong message as much as the spoken word. Vandeville warns British business people against the common British and American custom of beginning a meeting with a joke or light-hearted remark, for example. **This** could well create an unfavourable impression among clients used to a more formal business culture where work and play are kept apart.

Language work

1 In your own words, explain what is 'ironical' about the situation described in the UK.

2 Which word in paragraph 2 is used to indicate a rapid change?

3 Which phrase in paragraph 3 points to the importance of the secretary's role in the company?

UNIT 3

4   In your own words, explain why a telephone might be 'an intimidating instrument'. (line 31)

5   In your own words, explain why *Rendezvous* considers courses conducted over the telephone so effective.

6   Which word in paragraph 4 is used to mean 'a basic knowledge'?

7   Explain what you understand by the term 'acting out scenarios'. (line 47)

8   In your own words, explain the phrase 'to pass the time of day'. (line 50)

9   What is implied by the phrase 'dialogue of the deaf'? (line 56)

10 Which word in paragraph 6 describes a feeling of positive enjoyment?

11 In your own words, explain what is meant by the term 'body language'. (line 76)

12 What point does the example of the joke or light-hearted remark in paragraph 8 serve to illustrate?

Summary

In a paragraph of around **50–75 words**, explain in your own words the approach that secretaries should adopt towards learning languages, according to Anne Hamilton and Helen Vandeville.

Reference skills

Look back at these words and phrases which are in **bold** in the text. In each case say what each word or phrase is referring to. One has been done for you as an example.

    0 their (line 7)   =   *clients or colleagues*
    1 such skills (line 21)   =   _____
    2 it (line 33)   =   _____
    3 its (line 43)   =   _____
    4 same methods (line 48)   =   _____
    5 such an approach (line 56) =   _____
    6 such phrases (lines 58–59) =   _____
    7 this (line 81)   =   _____

Wordstress

1 Underline the stressed syllable on each of these words from the text.

1 secretary	5 colleague	9 consultant	13 immediacy	17 complicated
2 international	6 reputation	10 conducting	14 tuition	18 hospitality
3 communication	7 superficially	11 intimidating	15 necessarily	19 sensibility
4 organization	8 linguistic	12 instrument	16 exhilarating	20 potential

27

UNIT 3

2 Divide the words into groups according to their wordstress pattern. Practise saying the words to yourself.

▪▫ ▫▪▫ ▫▫▪▫ ▫▫▪▫▫ ▫▫▫▪▫
colleague _____ _____ _____ _____

▪▫▫ _____ ▫▪▫▫▫ _____ _____
_____ _____ _____ _____ _____

▪▫▫▫
_____

HELP WITH PUNCTUATION 3: Apostrophes and genitives

- The apostrophe is generally used to show that something has been omitted:
  in contractions   it is   →   it's
                     have not →   haven't
                     let us   →   let's

  N.B. Do not use apostrophes with pronouns:
  the city and its suburbs   _The fault was entirely hers._

- The apostrophe is also used to indicate possession:
  David's pen = a pen belonging to David
  David and Angela's car = a car belonging to both David and Angela

- When the possessor is plural, the apostrophe comes after the _s_:
  the teachers' room = a room used by a number of teachers

  N.B. With irregular plurals, the apostrophe comes before the _s_:
  the children's room = a room used by a number of children

- The apostrophe is generally used with nouns which refer to people, expressions of time and sometimes places, but is not used for objects:
  Wednesday's meeting of the club
  the door of Raymond's house
  London's excellent range of theatres

  N.B. _the door of the car_ or _the car door_

- The apostrophe is also used in some idiomatic phrases:
  I'm at my wit's end, I can't find a way out of this problem.

Add apostrophes to these sentences where needed.
1 Please dont waste everybody elses time as well as ours.
2 I havent bought anything for the twins birthday yet.
3 It isnt the sort of thing that suits Bill and Fionas taste.
4 The citys full of shops selling tomorrows fashions today.
5 Some childrens clothes are sold upstairs, others are to be found in teenage fashions.
6 Lindas appointment is at four oclock and Roberts follows hers, but youre not on todays list, Im afraid.
7 Well have to make sure that Mr Peters watch says the same time as ours.
8 Its high time the sports club did something about its members changing facilities.
9 Toms mothers house isnt as old as its appearance suggests, her neighbours houses are older.
10 Theirs is the villages most beautiful garden and theres no doubt its larger than anybody elses too.

GRAMMAR : The passive voice

Form: | to be + past participle of the main verb |

Use:
- when the active would have a 'weak' subject (someone, they, people, etc.):
  They had to close the motorway temporarily.
  *The motorway had to **be closed** temporarily.*

  People say it's an interesting play.
  *It**'s said** to be an interesting play.*

N.B. No agent *(by someone)* is needed in such sentences.

- to soften or avoid direct orders, accusations, quotes, etc.:
  You shouldn't have told Marianne.
  *Marianne shouldn't **have been told.***

  Someone has broken the door handle.
  *The door handle **has been broken**.*

  Our reporter says that there have been riots in country X.
  *Riots **have been reported** in country X.*

N.B. Such sentences shouldn't have an agent.

- when the action is more important than the agent, especially describing processes, etc.:
  A machine fits the pin into the slot.   *The postman has delivered a lot of letters.*
  *The pin **is fitted** into the slot mechanically.*   *A lot of letters **have been delivered**.*

N.B. Use the agent only when this is needed to give a full picture, compare:

  A bee chased Louise.   *Someone has left the gate open.*
  *Louise **was chased**...*   *The gate **has been left** open.*
  *Louise **was chased** by a bee.*

Finish each of the following sentences so that it is **as similar as possible in meaning to the sentence printed before it**, but uses the passive voice. Include an agent only where it is needed.

1   People say he is friendly with a number of well-known celebrities.
    He _____

2   People generally think that Paul did a good job.
    Paul _____

3   Most people consider Mr Jarvis to be the best dentist in town.
    Mr Jarvis _____

4   They are going to introduce a new law banning traffic from the city centre.
    A _____

5   An unnamed source alleges that the President is considering marriage.
    The _____

6   You have to leave the dough a couple of hours before baking it.
    The _____

7   They ought to have informed us that the train would be delayed.
    We _____

8   A large wasp distracted the students from the lecture.
    The _____

UNIT 3

9 Everyone believes that the wrong man was accused of the murder.
   The _____

10 I don't want anyone, for whatever reason, to touch the electricity meter.
   On no account _____

11 There is a rumour which says that the singer is planning to sell his house.
   The _____

12 Nobody had fixed a date for the meeting, so few people bothered to come.
   As no _____

MAKING SUGGESTIONS

Look at the three ways of using the verb *to suggest*:
   I suggest (that) you get a dog.
   I suggest (that) you should get a dog.
   I suggest getting a dog.

Rewrite each of the following sentences so that it is **as similar as possible in meaning to the sentence printed before it**, but uses a form of the verb to suggest.

   Example: 'Why don't you get a dog, John?' said Mary.
   Answer: _Mary suggested (that) John (should) get a dog._

1 'Why don't you join an animal welfare group, Tom?' said Melanie.
   _____

2 My suggestion would be for Terry to buy his own car.
   _____

3 Lyn has said that she thinks we should get a cat.
   _____

4 'Let's go to the cinema on Saturday night,' suggested Anna.
   _____

5 'I think you're working too hard, Wendy,' said Pat.
   _____

6 Darren says that we should go whale watching.
   _____

7 'I think it would be a good idea if Sharon started looking for a new job,' said Tracy.
   _____

8 'What about getting Grandma a tarantula for her birthday?' said Emma.
   _____

9 You should take up fishing, it's very relaxing.
   _____

10 'How about stopping for a cup of tea?' suggested Billy.
   _____

UNIT 3

HELP WITH SPELLING 3: Words ending in *y*

- You usually change a final *y* to *i* when adding a suffix:

    marr**y** → marr**i**age   earl**y** → earl**i**er
    beaut**y** → beaut**i**ful   da**y** → da**i**ly
    lonel**y** → lonel**i**ness

N.B. Do not change *y* when adding *-ing*:
    marr**y** → marr**y**ing   cop**y** → cop**y**ing

- You usually change *y* to *i* when forming plurals or adding the third person *s*:
    tr**y** → tr**i**es   beaut**y** → beaut**i**es

N.B. Do not change *y* if it is preceded by a single vowel:
    b**oy** → b**oy**s   p**ay** → p**ay**s   vall**ey** → vall**ey**s

1 Add a suffix to make nouns from these words.

1 rely	_____	6 lazy	_____
2 deny	_____	7 defy	_____
3 apply	_____	8 bully	_____
4 nasty	_____	9 dry	_____
5 imply	_____	10 lovely	_____

2 Make these singular nouns plural.

1 toy	_____	6 holiday	_____
2 trolley	_____	7 penny	_____
3 quarry	_____	8 display	_____
4 puppy	_____	9 spy	_____
5 highway	_____	10 fairy	_____

VOCABULARY: Similes

Choose **one** word from the box to complete the simile in each of the idiomatic phrases. One has been done for you as an example.

| black   peas   bright   quick   ~~dead~~   light   pretty   fresh   fit   stubborn   right |

0 There's no life left in that plant; it's as ___*dead*___ as a dodo.
1 Look at that old house; it's as _____ as a picture.
2 After a good long sleep, Edward felt as _____ as a daisy.
3 You have to be patient with Hilary, she's as _____ as a mule.
4 If you keep taking the medicine, you'll soon feel as _____ as rain.
5 After she'd taken out all the books, Muriel's bag felt as _____ as a feather.
6 I'm not surprised that Sharon's doing well at school, she's as _____ as a button.
7 David threw open the door and as _____ as a flash, made a grab for the jewel box.
8 After all that exercise I feel as _____ as a fiddle.
9 The brothers are as alike as two _____ in a pod.
10 I think it's going to rain; the sky to the west is as _____ as ink.

UNIT 3

USE OF ENGLISH: Cloze passage

In this passage, a recently successful novelist talks about her career. Choose **one** word from the box to put in each of the spaces in the passage. The words have been divided into categories to help you.

verbs:	~~grew~~, attracting, running, pick, stick
nouns:	affair, way
adverbs:	indeed, likely,
prepositions:	in, between, into, about
structure words:	who, should, do, not, since, were, one, as

My chequered career

As a child, I dreamed of being a writer when I (0) __grew__ up. The way I went (1) _____ realizing this was getting a job in publishing as a teenager. And to anyone (2) _____ thinks it's unfair that a literary agent (3) _____ have written a novel that's (4) _____ quite a lot of attention, I would say 'you can do it too. You too can go (5) _____ publishing at eighteen and type your (6) _____ through contracts and things for years, learning as you go'. But in truth, only now (7) _____ I feel I've got anything to write about. (8) _____, I think something would-be young writers tend to overlook is the fact that your first love (9) _____ as a student is fascinating to you, but (10) _____ necessarily to the world outside.

My great battle for the twenty years I've been (11) _____ my own literary agency has been to fight the distinction (12) _____ so-called literary and so-called commercial fiction. In my view, any novel now regarded (13) _____ a classic only has that status because it has sold well and continuously (14) _____ it was published. I was screamed down on television once for saying that, (15) _____ she to be writing today, Jane Austen would be writing just the sort of thing you (16) _____ up at airports. But I (17) _____ to my guns. A good story is (18) _____ which gets (19) _____ touch with a wider audience, the more it does so, the more (20) _____ it is to survive. So, why not be a good writer for people who pass through airports?

Comprehension

Decide if each of the statements **1–10** reflects what the writer feels by writing **Yes** or **No**.

1 It was always my ambition to become a writer. _____
2 I entered publishing at a secretarial level. _____
3 My first book was written when I was a student. _____
4 Writers need to have some experience of life. _____
5 It takes more than large sales to make a classic. _____
6 I have been criticised for writing 'commercial' fiction. _____
7 Some people disagreed with my comments about Jane Austen. _____
8 My writing was influenced by my knowledge of the publishing business. _____
9 It worries me that I may have an unfair advantage over other writers. _____
10 I used my job as a source of inspiration for plots and characters. _____

GRAMMAR: Comparison and contrast

For questions **1–12**, write one sentence that contains all the information in the two sentences printed above it and uses the word or expression in **bold** to form a comparison or contrast. The word or expression **must not be altered** in any way.

1. English makes great use of the passive.
   Some other European languages do not.
   unlike

2. Computers save a lot of time.
   Learning how to use a computer can be very time consuming.
   although

3. The demand for cookery books is rising.
   The demand for quiz books remains stable.
   whilst

4. Our local bus service is very regular.
   Other areas are not so lucky.
   comparison

5. It rained heavily for a short time.
   The garden party was a great success.
   despite

6. Many people think eating out in Glasgow is expensive.
   Prices are actually quite reasonable.
   far from

7. James had a slight head cold.
   He sang beautifully at Jessica's wedding.
   in spite of

8. The coach takes five hours to get to London.
   The train does it in two and a half hours.
   whereas

9. You may dislike folk music very much.
   I'm sure you'll like this particular band.
   however

10. Hill walking is tiring.
    Mountain climbing requires more concentration.
    as much

11. I know you're not keen on Italian food.
    I think you should at least try a piece of polenta.
    nonetheless

12. My car is not easy to drive.
    Yours demands more skill of the driver.
    the same degree

UNIT 3

WRITING: Translations

Look at this translation into English from another language. In each line there is one mistake of either grammar or vocabulary. In each case:

- identify the mistake by underlining it
- write a correction of the underlined part in the space
- say what type of mistake this is

To make <u>it</u> possible the opening of the old house　　(0) omit *it*
to the public, <u>mayor</u> works of restoration　　(0) major (spelling)
have been carried <u>away</u> in recent months.　　(0) out (*away* = wrong preposition)
Some cracks in the old structure they were　　(1) _____
in urgent need to repair. The staircases　　(2) _____
had to be renewed and up-to-dated in order　　(3) _____
to conform at modern fire regulations. All　　(4) _____
parts of the house are now fernished in period style.　　(5) _____
The house is open up the public as follows:　　(6) _____
Visits can to be made from 10 am to 5 pm.　　(7) _____
Only ten persons for a time can enter the house.　　(8) _____
The lenght of one visit is fixed at 30 minutes.　　(9) _____
The prize of the ticket is $2 for adults, children　　(10) _____
till one metre in height $1 and old-age pensioners　　(11) _____
$1, (those living in the city are admited free).　　(12) _____

WRITING: An article

You have been asked to write an article for a student magazine on the topic of translating into English. Write a short article of about 150 words in which you talk about:

- common problems encountered when translating from your language in to English
- suggestions on how to avoid the most common mistakes
- suggestions of books, materials, etc. that might be useful

Before writing, think about your readers:

What information will be useful for them?
How can you make the article interesting as well as informative?
What style should the article be written in?

UNIT 4

A Fine Romance

VOCABULARY: Wordsearch

1 Find as many adjectives and nouns to describe people's character as you can in the grid. Words may run horizontally or vertically. One has been done for you as an example.

```
M O D E S T Y V B R A V E R
C A U T I O U S B T A S K E
O X X W I S E C R L O Y A L
M E E I P L O V I N G I O I
M I N T E L L I G E N C E A
O W E T R U S T H Y I X B B
N A S Y H E R O T O C H U I
S T Y L E M N H P U E P L L
E S I A N M O O D Y D A L I
N O S Y P O U N N A S T Y T
S E X Y G E N E R O S I T Y
E B O S S Y I S O I U E L M
D F T A L E N T E D M N D F
O I U S U L K Y W E R C O I
C H A R M J U D G E M E N T
```

2 Divide the words you have found into these four categories, then make nouns from the adjectives and adjectives from the nouns. One has been done for you as an example.

Positive adjectives	(nouns)	Positive nouns	(adjectives)
loving	*love/lover*		

Negative adjectives	(nouns)	Negative nouns	(adjectives)

35

UNIT 4

READING

Read this article carefully and for questions **1–5**, choose the best alternative **A**, **B**, **C** or **D** which fits best.

The agony and the ecstasy

Summer, traditional time of moonlight and romance, is in the air and bookshops are busting out all over with advice for those whose path is strewn with briars. Agony aunts, marriage counsellors and psychologists have rushed into paroxysm of print: how to have a good relationship, stay together, solve your problems, how to understand the opposite sex. They are the relationship experts, dispensing understanding and advice to anyone who has hit a bad patch.

To write about the pursuit of happiness is brave; to offer guidance is braver still. It betokens a confidence in their own opinion that some might call foolhardy. One cannot but ask who are these self-styled authorities? Do agony aunts manage their lives and loves with equal perception and professionalism, or is a fair share of strife essential to sympathy?

Irma Kurtz makes no bones about calling herself an agony aunt. Hers is the common-sense counsel of an outspoken friend, freely dished-out to thousands of readers in one of Britain's top women's magazines. She claims no formal training, no favourite philosophy, no know-it-all dogma. As Irma says, 'Endless curiosity and an irrepressible compulsion to communicate what I'm thinking are probably the two highest qualifications for this job. Nosy and bossy in other words.'

That and empathy. Irma – wise, warm, funny, tolerant – is the first to admit how many of the problems which arrive in her postbag strike a chord, the last to take the moral high ground. 'I too, have been there in my time, and, more than once, believe me, made a mess of things,' she writes in her book, *Ten-point Plan for an Untroubled Life*. 'I've sent letters I wished I hadn't in my time,' she confides, 'I have been out with men I did not really love and loved men I did not really like much.'

She is 59, and now relishes the richness of life in a tiny flat in London's West End; theatres and restaurants only a heartbeat away. The ten-point plan is a self-help book, she says. 'It's very important to have the confidence to solve your own problems and not immediately cry "help", because no one is more expert in your own experience than you, and I really think we are forgetting that.'

'I didn't expect to be on my own at 60 I never cared about marriage, but I always believed I'd find this great love.' Twice she was deeply in love; 'The first time and the last time, like bookends. With the last one, ten years ago, I remember thinking, "Dear God, just get me out of this in one piece and I'll never do it again, never."'

But this, as she is keen to point out, is only her experience, 'You can't assume that it will be everyone's; all it teaches you is the variety and possibility of life'. If there is one vital lesson to pass on, she says, it would be the importance of the essential. 'Keep in view what matters to you – be it friendships, love or whatever – and don't let silly things get in the way. Listen to the music and ignore the static.'

Comprehension

1   In the introduction, what point is the writer making about the type of book she mentions?
   A   Sales are booming at the moment.
   B   They are attracting a lot of publicity.
   C   Some new titles have just appeared.
   D   Some surprising people are writing them.

2   The writer expresses a doubt about whether the people who write these books
   A   have sufficient experience.
   B   are suitably qualified.
   C   lead happy lives themselves.
   D   really understand the problems of others.

3 Irma Kurtz's approach can be described as based on
   A   certain guiding principles.
   B   interest in other people.
   C   research into human behaviour.
   D   a keen sense of humour.

4 Irma Kurtz admits that
   A   she has made mistakes in her life.
   B   she often turns to others for help.
   C   she is dissatisfied with her present life.
   D   she regrets not getting married.

5 What is Irma's principal piece of advice to people?
   A   Be open to life's possibilities.
   B   Don't look to others for help.
   C   Don't let love pass you by.
   D   Know your own priorities.

Vocabulary

Find these words and expressions in the text. Paragraph numbers are given in brackets and one has been done for you as an example.

0	an idiomatic phrase meaning *full of* (1)	*busting out all over*
1	a verb meaning *to give out* (1)	
2	a verb meaning *to suggest* (2)	
3	an adjective meaning *unwise* (2)	
4	a noun meaning *difficulty* (2)	
5	an idiomatic phrase which means *doesn't hesitate to admit* (3)	
6	an adjective meaning *frank and honest* (3)	
7	a phrasal verb meaning *given* (3)	
8	a noun meaning *a set of fixed ideas* (3)	
9	an adjective meaning *unstoppable* (3)	
10	an idiomatic phrase meaning *remind (one) of something* (4)	
11	a verb meaning *to enjoy very much* (5)	
12	two adjectives both meaning *very important* (7)	

Wordstress

Mark the wordstress on these words from the article.

1	counsellor	5	professionalism	9	compulsion
2	psychologist	6	curiosity	10	qualifications
3	relationship	7	outspoken	11	unbelievably
4	perception	8	irrepressible	12	essential

Summary

In a paragraph of **75–100 words**, summarize Irma Kurtz's attitude towards problems in relationships and say whether you agree with it or not.

UNIT 4

NARRATIVE DEVICES: Inversion

Inversion is a narrative device used to give emphasis to one aspect of the sentence:
He had no sooner got under the shower than the phone rang.
No sooner had he got under the shower than the phone rang.

The second, inverted sentence emphasises the irony of the situation by placing the negative adverbial expression (*no sooner*) at the beginning. This is followed by the inversion of subject and auxiliary. When the original sentence has no auxiliary, use *do*:
You very rarely meet couples who never argue.
*Very rarely **do** you meet couples who never argue.*

Rewrite each of the following sentences so that it is **as similar as possible in meaning to the sentence printed before it**, but begins with a negative adverbial. One has been done for you as an example.

0 I little realized how much they were in love.
   Little did I realise how much they were in love.

1 One seldom gets the chance to meet famous writers.

2 The bus will no longer stop outside the Post Office.

3 I hardly ever stop to count the number of cups of coffee I drink.

4 John had hardly had time to take his seat in the cinema when the lights went out.

5 You scarcely ever see owls during the daytime.

6 I have never experienced such an uncomfortable journey in my whole life.

7 You don't often get offered an opportunity like that.

8 This envelope shouldn't be opened under any circumstances.

9 As he walked into the town, Richard didn't meet a soul.

10 I only realized what I'd said when I saw the look on her face.

HELP WITH SPELLING 4: Common errors

Some pairs of words which sound the same, or very similar, are often confused:

principle	→	a general law or truth
principal	→	most important thing or person
a brake	→	it stops your car or bicycle
a break	→	It's an interval or something's broken
advice	→	it's a noun
advise	→	it's a verb

38

Choose the correct spelling from the alternatives in brackets in each of these sentences.

1. I think we have to go back to first (*principles/principals*) to understand this problem.
2. There's been a (*brake/break*) in at the shop, lots of money has been stolen.
3. Let me give you some (*advice/advise*).
4. For (*dessert/desert*) there is either ice-cream or fruit salad.
5. Be careful not to (*loose/lose*) your button, it looks a bit (*loose/lose*) to me.
6. Tanya has put in hours of (*practise/practice*) since getting her own piano.
7. The traffic was completely (*stationery/stationary*) during the hold up on the motorway.
8. I can't decide (*weather/whether*) to take an umbrella today.
9. It was (*quiet/quite*) a nice skirt, but not really what Sarah was looking for.
10. We (*past/passed*) John's old school on the way to the bank.
11. The building had (*formally/formerly*) been used as a barn before being turned into a house.
12. I thought I recognized the man who came and sat (*beside/besides*) me on the bus.

Do you know what the other words mean? Use your dictionary to check.

USE OF ENGLISH: Cloze passage

Fill each of the numbered spaces in the passage with **one** suitable word. One has been done for you as an example.

Anger

Anger can get us into hot water – and bottling things up only makes matters worse. But you can do more than simply gnash your teeth.

Anger is (**0**) __*one*__ of the most commonly felt emotions, yet relatively few of us know how to cope (**1**) _____ it effectively. Shouting, swearing, and hitting inanimate objects are common responses (**2**) _____ the age-old problem of expressing our often accumulated frustrations. Nevertheless, losing control is more (**3**) _____ to lead to humiliation than vindication.

So, we learn not to lose control. In public, our tension is held (**4**) _____ check by the urge to (**5**) _____ on to our dignity, whilst the extent of our reaction to any event will (**6**) _____ on unresolved issues from the past. People tend to carry learned responses, so if parents scream or fall (**7**) _____ awkward silences when they are cross, their offspring will probably (**8**) _____ the same.

Conversely, a child may be terrified (**9**) _____ anger because one of its parents had no control over their temper. As a result, the child may repress (**10**) _____ own feelings, often expressing them inappropriately or channelling them internally (**11**) _____ thus feeling depressed. In fact, depression is often (**12**) _____ 'internal anger'.

Self-expression is the key to dealing with anger. (**13**) _____ there are no hard and fast rules for (**14**) _____ best to achieve this, burying the debris is probably (**15**) _____ least productive method. Physical release through exercise can be effective – even working (**16**) _____ at the gym may help.

Strange (**17**) _____ it sounds, I've seen tension in relationships evaporate through pillow or water fights. In (**18**) _____ emergency, shouting in a parked car, or hitting a pillow with a tied towel are also good (**19**) _____ of relief, although these methods are considerably less demure (**20**) _____ writing it all down in a diary.

UNIT 4

Writing: a narrative

Write a story of around 150 words describing a time when you got really angry.

Think about:
- what made you angry in the first place
- how your anger grew
- how you expressed your anger
- how people responded
- how you felt afterwards

Remember these expressions:

to bottle things up	to gnash your teeth
to hit the roof	to blow your top
to lose your temper	to seethe with rage
to lose control	my blood boiled

VOCABULARY: Uses of *get*

- *Get* is a commonly used verb, especially in spoken language.

- *Get* is often used instead of *become*:
  I'm getting tired, let's stop for a rest.

- *Get* is often found in passive constructions:
  Henry got mugged on his way home last night.

- *Get* is often used in phrasal verbs:
  Tim and Sandra are getting on very well together.

- *Get* is often used in a reflexive sense:
  It's time we got (ourselves) organized and planned our holiday.

Rewrite each of the following sentences so that it is **as similar as possible in meaning to the sentence printed before it**, but uses a form of the verb *to get*.

Example: I hope your health improves soon.
Answer: _I hope you get better soon._

1. Tom and Carly were married on Saturday.

2. Jane was blamed for the mistake.

3. Rosy is very easily upset.

4. I would like to be friendlier with my neighbours.

5. Susan yawned because she was finding the play boring.

6. Terry's teacher told him off yesterday.

7. During the fight, someone broke a large window.

8. After ten minutes, waiting began to depress Kathy.

9. Peter was finding Sally's behaviour increasingly annoying.

10. Simon should have that broken tooth looked at by a dentist.

GRAMMAR: Structure words

Read this review of a new series of art books. A number of structure words have been taken out. From the alternatives in italics, choose the correct form or the word which fits best in the context of the passage.

History of Art

This major new series aims to present major chunks of world art history in a way that is popular and enticing (**1**) *without/avoiding* being bland, unquestioning and patronising to (**2**) *ones/those* who can already tell Manet from Monet.

The first five titles are coming out as a group. (**3**) *Each/All* are flawlessly designed and sensitively organized, with reader-friendly notes, glossary and index. (**4**) *This/Such* realistic approach extends to the price – at £8.99 each, you can afford, or (**5**) *while/at least* be tempted, to buy in bulk – (**6**) *especially/simply* when you compare these with similar art history books, costing far more.

(**7**) *Although/However* attractive its packaging, a series like this risks being over-ambitious; it can't simply rewrite the whole history of art in one fell swoop, as one over-excited critic, quoted on each jacket, has claimed. There is (**8**) *only/hardly* so much you can say in two hundred pages when there are almost as many images which must be interpreted and contextualized to give a bigger picture, especially (**9**) *when/whether* dealing with a subject, for example, as vast as 'Art in China'.

(**10**) *Yet/Whilst* the authors, invariably experts in their fields, manage to juggle their own and other people's opinions with enviable wit, and without losing less-informed readers. (**11**) *However/Despite* the rigid format, these are books with personality as well as looks – there is simply no other art history series as wide-ranging, well-researched and up-to-date. (**12**) *But/And* it is fair to say that the publishers cannot be accused of cutting corners; there are another fifty-five volumes to come.

Language work

Look at these two phrases from the review:

All are flawlessly designed and sensitively organized with reader-friendly notes.

However attractive its packaging, a series like this risks being over-ambitious.

1 How many pieces of information or opinion does each include?

2 What references are there to things outside the sentence? How are these made?

3 How are the pieces of information linked together?

4 Where do you expect to find this style of writing?

5 Why is it so effective?

6 Find some more examples of noun phrases in the review.

UNIT 4

HELP WITH PUNCTUATION 4: Inverted commas

Inverted commas are used:

- when we write the actual words which somebody said
- in dialogues in a narrative
- when we quote words or phrases
- when we use slang, technical terms, etc.:

'Hang on a moment' I said.
Jerry walked in and said, 'Hello everybody. What's been going on?'
The whole 'dog hair thing,' as Kendall calls it.
All these pets are 'harmless', 'friendly' even.

N.B. Other punctuation marks usually come inside the inverted commas.

Add all the necessary punctuation to this short piece of narrative.

Robert looked down at the hole in his pullover what am I going to tell auntie he said tell her you lost it I suggested shell knit you another Robert didnt look convinced and was trying to take off the remains of his pullover hang on a moment I said ill help you I hadnt heard footsteps or the gate opening but suddenly I heard miss Lockes voice enquiring icily what on earth is going on here

USE OF ENGLISH: Cloze passage

Fill each of the numbered spaces in this article about a bird sanctuary with **one** suitable word. One has been done for you as an example.

Are you searching for some tranquillity? Whether you're looking to escape (**0**) ___*from*___ civilization for a few hours or completely submerge (**1**) _____ in nature, we've found the perfect place, Peakirk Gardens. Here, you can replace city noise (**2**) _____ birdsong or swap the hustle and bustle (**3**) _____ a slow walk around peaceful gardens.

Founded (**4**) _____ Sir Peter Scott, the renowned naturalist, Peakirk has been a haven for birds for over thirty years. Each species has an area of its (**5**) _____ which has been painstakingly copied from various habitats (**6**) _____ the wild. For endangered species, even more care is (**7**) _____, including special diets and closely-monitored egg production. Newly (**8**) _____ eggs are often removed from the mother and incubated, therefore increasing their (**9**) _____ of survival.

The birds are also well protected by a chain-link fence which (**10**) _____ the park and is regularly patrolled. In the past, (**11**) _____ have been problems with predators. It (**12**) _____ be heartbreaking if all the hard work that goes (**13**) _____ protecting a species were to be wiped (**14**) _____ by a hungry fox, for example.

And it isn't (**15**) _____ rare or endangered species that home in (**16**) _____ Peakirk. Thousands of migrating birds use it (**17**) _____ a stopover before flying on to their next port of call. But even (**18**) _____ you are someone for (**19**) _____ all birds look alike, Peakirk offers a tranquil retreat where the pace of life slows right (**20**) _____ from a sprint to a gentle stroll.

Writing: a formal letter

You decide to write a letter to the warden of Peakirk Gardens to see if it is possible to do some voluntary work there. The letter should be between 150 and 200 words in length.

In your letter:
- introduce yourself
- say how you heard about the sanctuary
- ask about voluntary work
- say when you're available and how you might be useful

IDIOMATIC EXPRESSIONS

For each of the sentences, write a new sentence **as similar as possible in meaning to the original sentence**, but using the word given. This word **must not be altered** in any way. Try to use a form of the verb *to get* if possible.

1 When she talks about herself like that it really irritates me.
 nerves

2 I find all this talk of marital disharmony very depressing.
 down

3 I think we'll have to hurry up if we're going to catch that bus.
 move

4 Renata enjoys looking after young children very much.
 gets

5 I don't seem to be able to understand this instruction booklet.
 head

6 David doesn't seem to able to get on top of the new computer system.
 grips

7 Angela is just recovering from a nasty bout of flu.
 over

8 Maggie's little boy is just learning to put on his own clothes.
 dressed

9 That little joke really caused a lot of trouble for me.
 water

10 Molly finds it difficult to accept the idea that her daughter is grown up.
 used

UNIT 5

All Right on the Night

READING: Pre-reading task

Look at the first paragraph of this text. Read it quickly. One phrasal verb is used four times in this paragraph. Can you find it? What does it mean?

Use of the article

Look at the first paragraph more closely and put an article, either *a*, *an* or *the* in each of the spaces **1–16**. One has been done for you as an example.

Who's a pretty plant then?

Plants are named after the great and (**0**) __*the*__ good, the worthy and (**1**) _____ wealthy. Indeed, one of (**2**) _____ greatest honours that can be bestowed upon anyone is to have (**3**) _____ plant named after **them**. Sometimes (**4**) _____ person is famous and (**5**) _____ naming of (**6**) _____ plant is (**7**) _____ natural succession to popularity and public acclaim. Actors, singers, dancers, royalty, and latterly
5 even (**8**) _____ television news-reader, have all been honoured by having (**9**) _____ plant named after them. On occasion, (**10**) _____ individual has had no public profile, but (**11**) _____ plant has become popular so that we feel we know them. Few people are likely to recognize (**12**) _____ name of Maria Ann Smith, but most will have heard of (**13**) _____ apple named after her, (**14**) _____ famous Granny Smith; (**15**) _____ case of the plant making (**16**) _____ person famous.

Now read the rest of the article and for questions **17–28**, choose the word or phrase **A**, **B** or **C** which fits best in each of the spaces.

10 In years gone by, it was not always easy to determine that a plant had been named in honour of a person, because the name became Latinized. **This** was, (**17**) _____ considered to be very chic, (**18**) _____ surely only a socialite or an academic would have known that the *Lilium mackliniae* immortalized Jean Macklin, the wife of a famous botanist.

In recent times, **this practice** has died out and now when a plant is named after a person it is clear for
15 everyone to see. The beautiful patio rose Anna Ford, (**19**) _____ is a fitting tribute to the broadcaster, (**20**) _____ former Nottingham Forest football manager, Brian Clough, is feted with a luminous salmon-orange exhibition sweet pea.

(**21**) _____ who decides upon those who should be honoured in **such a way**? There are no hard and fast rules. (**22**) _____ for the most part, plants are named by their breeders or originators, either as an honour to
20 someone near and dear, or as a mark of respect for the famous. But there are commercial undertones. If you

can launch a new rose named after a really popular celebrity at a flower show and get **that person** to attend, then the press coverage received is enormous.

_____ (23), if you decide to name your sweet pea after Barry Dare, the former Managing Director of your company, as Unwins Seeds of Cambridge did recently, then the commercial value is little. _____ (24), the
25 honour for **the person concerned** is great, recognizing as it does strong leadership, hard work and the affection of the staff.

If nobody is interested in naming a plant after you, _____ (25) it is always possible to buy a new variety and have it named yourself. **This** is common practice amongst commercial companies, especially with roses, **where** names like ,'Typhoo Tea', 'Benson and Hedges Gold' and 'Yorkshire Bank' serve as good
30 advertisements. If you can come up with the cash, then you can buy the name rights to a new unnamed variety and name it after **yourself** or a member of your family.

However, _____ (26) some varieties like the peony Sarah Bernhardt live on for a century or more and seemed destined to last for ever, _____ (27) disappear within a couple of years, never to be seen again, _____ (28) they bear a famous name. If the plant proves inferior to those already on the market, then it
35 generally takes more than a famous name to save **it**.

17	A	however	B	for example	C	therefore
18	A	otherwise	B	but	C	despite
19	A	for example	B	however	C	on the other hand
20	A	indeed	B	when	C	while
21	A	So	B	Although	C	Likewise
22	A	But	B	For instance	C	If
23	A	Therefore	B	On the other hand	C	Otherwise
24	A	However	B	Providing	C	Despite
25	A	therefore	B	however	C	then
26	A	whilst	B	when	C	because
27	A	others	B	these	C	all
28	A	whether	B	unless	C	even if

Reference skills

Look back at these words and phrases which are in **bold** in the text. In each case say what each word or phrase is referring to. One has been done for you as an example.

0	them (line 3)	=	*anyone*
1	this (line 11)	=	_____
2	this practice (line 14)	=	_____
3	such a way (line 18)	=	_____
4	that person (line 21)	=	_____
5	the person concerned (line 25)	=	_____
6	this (line 28)	=	_____
7	where (line 29)	=	_____
8	yourself (line 31)	=	_____
9	it (line 35)	=	_____

UNIT 5

Vocabulary

Look back at the extract and find words that mean the following. Paragraph numbers are given in brackets and one has been done for you as an example.

0 a verb meaning to give *someone an honour* (1)	*bestow*
1 a noun meaning *approval* (1)	_____
2 an adverb meaning *recently* (1)	_____
3 a phrase meaning *sometimes* (1)	_____
4 a phrase meaning *in the past* (2)	_____
5 an adjective meaning *stylish* (2)	_____
6 an adjective meaning *appropriate* (3)	_____
7 a verb meaning *honoured* (3)	_____
8 a phrase meaning *fixed* (4)	_____
9 a phrase meaning *find the money* (6)	_____

Summary

Write a paragraph of about **75 words** explaining the various ways by which a new plant might get its name. Use your own words as far as is possible.

GRAMMAR: Clauses with *whatever, however* etc.

Finish each of the following sentences so that it is **as similar as possible in meaning to the sentence printed before it.**

Example: I don't care what you say, she's a wonderful actress.
Answer: Whatever *you (may) say, she's a wonderful actress.*

1 Whatever it may cost, I'm determined to complete the project.
   However _____
2 It may make him unpopular, but John always sticks to his principles.
   However _____
3 If you do nothing else while you're in London, go to the National Gallery.
   Whatever _____
4 She has appeared in many films, but always seems to play the same character.
   Whatever _____
5 It doesn't matter which road you take, they all end up at the same place.
   Whichever _____
6 It doesn't matter where you go in the city, you see wonderful examples of modern architecture.
   Wherever _____
7 I'm reminded of Marilyn Monroe every time I see Sally in that dress.
   Whenever _____
8 Ask as many people as you like, I'm sure you'll get the same answer.
   However _____

UNIT 5

SPELLING AND PRONUNCIATION

1 Complete each of the sentences with **one** word from the box.

| though   through   thought   throughout |
| thorough   tough   troughs   distraught |

1 He was always a very _____ person, no stone was ever left unturned.
2 It doesn't matter how much you spend on a present, it's the _____ that counts.
3 I'm sorry, Mr Jones is not in the office today, could I put you _____ to his secretary?
4 It's rather _____ on Marion, having to walk all that way with such a heavy bag.
5 The history of the business has really been a long series of peaks and _____.
6 _____ the match, Tracy tried not to think about what she would do with the prize money if she won.
7 The young couple looked very _____ when they learned that their new car had been stolen.
8 Tired _____ he was, Mike was determined to cycle to the next village before nightfall.

2 Put the words in the box into one of three lists, according to how the final sound is pronounced. The words in each list should rhyme with one of the words below the box.

| taught   draught   sought   trough   enough   ought   fraught |
| tough   laughed   nought   rough   coughed   caught   distraught |

port /pɔːt/   **craft** /krɑːft/   **stuff** /stʌf/
_____   _____   _____
_____   _____   _____
_____   _____   _____
_____
_____
_____

3 Some words sound the same, but have different spellings depending on the meaning. For each sentence, choose the correct form from the alternatives given. One has been done for you as an example.

0 He *sighted*/*cited* an old textbook as his main source of reference.
1 What *sort*/*sought* of car will you buy next?
2 The tennis players walked on to the *caught*/*court* just after 2 o'clock.
3 They arrived at the race *course*/*coarse* just in time to see the first race.
4 The weather was really *fowl*/*foul*, so they turned back after a while.
5 Jason is hoping to become the next teenage pop *idle*/*idol*.
6 Knowing that the burglar alarm was fitted to the house, gave the family great *piece*/*peace* of mind when they were away on holiday.
7 Her son's appearance on TV was a great *sauce*/*source* of pride for Mrs Berkeley.
8 Sharon has been to choose the *bridal*/*bridle* gown for her wedding next Spring.
9 The cinema was so full that people were sitting in the *isle*/*aisle*.
10 I can't *bear*/*bare* to see scenes of violence on TV. I have to switch it off.
11 Melanie is researching recent trends in air *fairs*/*fares* between the two cities.
12 Don't buy that trashy magazine, it's a complete *waist*/*waste* of money.

Do you know what the other words mean? Use a dictionary to check.

UNIT 5

GRAMMAR: Reported speech

- When reported speech is introduced with a verb in the past tense, most of the verbs used in the direct speech version change to agree with that verb:
  'I am tired,' Tony said.
  Tony said he was tired.

  'Is it raining, Helen?' asked Tony
  Tony asked Helen if it was raining.

  'I can't come on Friday,' Milly explained
  Milly explained that she couldn't come on Friday.

- As a general rule all present verb tenses change to past verb tenses and all past verb tenses change to the past perfect tense:
  'Sally went to London last year,' Tom said to Mary.
  Tom told Mary that Sally had been to London the previous year.

  'Have you ever met Chris?' Graham asked Polly.
  Polly asked Graham if she had ever met Chris.

N.B. Past perfect tenses and past modals do not change.
  'I hadn't thought of that,' admitted John.
  John admitted that he hadn't thought of that.

  'Would you like a coffee, David?' asked Wendy.
  Wendy asked David if he'd like a coffee.

1 Finish each of the following sentences so that it is **as similar as possible in meaning to the sentence printed before it.**

0 'The woman is tall and slim with a dark complexion,' Tanya said to the police officer.
Tanya told _the police officer that the woman was tall and slim with a dark complexion._

1 'Do you know Mr Trout's phone number, Liz?' asked Darren.
Darren _____

2 'What time did the fight start?' the reporter asked the woman.
The _____

3 'How's your sister getting on at her new school, Mandy?' asked Tracy.
Tracy _____

4 'Could you pass me the newspaper please, Patty,' said her father.
Patty's _____

5 'I'm having my car serviced tomorrow, so I can't give you a lift,' Peter explained to Rosie.
Peter _____

6 'I think it's going to be a day to remember,' said the sports commentator.
The _____

7 'I'll have to ring you back later, Tom, there's somebody knocking at the door,' said William.
William _____

8 'I'm sorry, but could you repeat your surname please, Sir,' said the receptionist.
The _____

9 'Can you get Josie to ring me after lunch, please Terry?' said Fiona.
Fiona _____

UNIT 5

2 Rewrite each of the sentences so that it is **as similar as possible in meaning to the sentence printed before it**.

0   Vanessa said that she was still very sleepy after that long flight.
    'I'm still very sleepy after that long flight,' said Vanessa.

1   The reporter asked the woman who had been mugged to tell him exactly what had happened.

2   The police officer asked Mrs Hilary how many times she had answered the phone that evening.

3   Phil asked Sharon if she would like to go to the party with him.

4   I asked Denise whether she was enjoying her new job.

5   I explained to the band that I couldn't sing that night as I'd just had a tooth out.

6   Annette asked Mike how long it would take to get to the cinema.

7   Richard said he was very disappointed that no one had asked his opinion.

8   Diane asked Mr French why she hadn't been invited to last week's meeting.

9   Simon said that he would like to thank all those who had sent him good wishes during his illness last year.

VOCABULARY: Wordsearch

Find as many words as possible connected with the topic of entertainment and the arts as you can in the grid. Words may run horizontally or vertically. One has been done for you as an example.

```
C O M E D Y X J X X P L O T
A R I X A X M A D R A M A H
R O M A N C E Z H O R R O R
T C E X C P D Z X T X X X I
O K X Y E O I T T D I S C L
O P E R A P A M U S I C A L
N T R A D E G Y X C X Y T E
C H A R A C T E R O S C A R
D I R E C T O R X S T Y L E
G P H X T F O L K T U I O I
E L E V I D E O X U D M G N
N A R R A T I V E M I A U E
R Y O S T A G E X E O G E M
E P E R F O R M A N C E X A
```

Can you remember any more words connected with entertainments and the arts?

49

UNIT 5

WRITING: Cloze passage

Read the article and choose the best word **A**, **B**, **C** or **D** for each of the numbered spaces. One has been done for you as an example.

Grease is not such a smash hit

The trouble with many London restaurants is that more planning seems to have gone into what's on the walls than into what goes on the plates. And, sadly, that is what has (**0**) __*B*__ wrong with the new restaurant called *Grease*.

It (**1**) _____ a lot, which is what you'd expect from the owner, Johnny Price who, after all, has created a number of fabulously fashionable eating places around the city. He's certainly been clever in (**2**) _____ *Grease*. As you walk into the two-storey building, you feel (**3**) _____ you're back in the 1970s. Plastered on the walls are advertising images from that decade, the floors are covered (**4**) _____ hexagonal tiles and the seating is mostly built-in circular sofas.

But (**5**) _____ of all, at the back of the restaurant, behind a glass wall, are the gleaming tanks of a working brewery. Four (**6**) _____ of the beer are on sale and it's not bad! It's certainly a fun environment that makes a good talking (**7**) _____ throughout the meal.

My dinner (**8**) _____ off to an excellent start, with an appetiser of wood-roasted vegetables. But for the main course, I made the (**9**) _____ of ordering a salmon dish. It took more than an hour before it arrived. My dining partner, himself a chef, took one (**10**) _____ and told me it was off. I sliced into it and sure (**11**) _____, it seemed undercooked. I sent it back and when it (**12**) _____ to reappear after another thirty minutes, settled for a pizza (**13**) _____ with mozzarella, pesto and rocket. It was delicious.

Surprisingly pleasant also was my dessert of basil and mascarpone ice-cream with stewed rhubarb. In the end, (**14**) _____ , dinner had taken three times longer than it should have done. The only taste in my mouth when I saw the bill was a bitter one. Our meal for two (**15**) _____ to the princely sum of £62 without service.

0	A been	B gone	C become	D got
1	A promises	B expects	C anticipates	D threatens
2	A the design	B to design	C designing	D design of
3	A how	B through	C like	D as
4	A with	B by	C from	D on
5	A strangest	B stranger	C strangely	D strange
6	A branches	B varieties	C strains	D sorts
7	A time	B focus	C piece	D point
8	A took	B got	C went	D started
9	A fool	B mistake	C choice	D fuss
10	A stink	B sneeze	C sniff	D snout
11	A enough	B to truth	C to form	D be
12	A wanted	B failed	C happened	D waited
13	A topped	B soaked	C spread	D sliced
14	A despite	B moreover	C therefore	D however
15	A arrived	B came	C reached	D got

UNIT 5

COMPREHENSION

1 Say whether these statements are **True** or **False**, according to the writer's opinion.

1 I thought the restaurant was going to be very good. _____
2 The appearance of the restaurant is very impressive. _____
3 The brewery is an unnecessary distraction. _____
4 Most of the food I ordered was disappointing. _____
5 I felt that the service could have been better. _____
6 The restaurant offers good value for money. _____

2 What rating out of ten do you think the writer would have given the restaurant under these headings?

1 decor _____ 2 service _____ 3 food _____ 4 drink _____ 5 value _____

3 What is the topic of each paragraph?

1 _____ 3 _____ 5 _____
2 _____ 4 _____

4 In each paragraph, what is the balance between:

A description of the restaurant and food?
B the writer's opinion of the restaurant and food?

1 _____ 3 _____ 5 _____
2 _____ 4 _____

5 Where would you expect to find a piece of writing like this?

6 Who do you think is likely to read it?

7 How would you describe the style in which it is written?

WRITING: a review

You have been asked by a local English language magazine which is read by English-speaking visitors and residents in your home area, to write a review of two different restaurants; one which you would recommend and one which you would not. You should write about 150-200 words.

Think about:
- your target readers
- what they want to know
- the style you should adopt
- how to make the review interesting

Which is best, two separate reviews or one longer piece which compares the two places?

In a longer piece:
What kind of language could you use to make comparisons?
How would the paragraphs be organized?

UNIT 5

USE OF ENGLISH: Cloze passage

Put **one** word in each of the spaces in this passage. One has been done for you as an example.

Pets on sets

Have you ever thought that your pet (**0**) ___*might*___ have star potential? (**1**) _____ Hollywood films and TV commercials to bit parts in soap operas, there are plenty of opportunities (**2**) _____ animals in the acting world. The agencies are deluged (**3**) _____ people wanting to get their pet on television. For pets are (**4**) _____ babies, everyone thinks that theirs is the best.

The industry is divided (**5**) _____ two main categories. The top five percent of animal actors are called 'the heroes'. They are the stars, the ones (**6**) _____ do the high profile TV work because they'll sit anywhere and do anything. (**7**) _____ for the majority there is only (**8**) _____ is called 'atmosphere' work. A dog may be required to jog along a beach with an actor, for example, (**9**) _____ maybe just sit on a sofa. Such work isn't brilliantly paid.

Agencies will source, train and supervise any species, with the exception (**10**) _____ wild animals. Most animals with star roles (**11**) _____ time with an agency trainer before filming. It (**12**) _____ one trainer six weeks to get a duck called Joseph to walk on set and pick (**13**) _____ a packet of crisps in an advertisement. The duck had to get (**14**) _____ to lights and noises, so as (**15**) _____ to be frightened in the studio.

Top animal stars can earn (**16**) _____ excess of £1000 per day, but the work (**17**) _____ to come in dribs and drabs rather than regularly. And if your pet (**18**) _____ land the star role, don't despair. Two understudies trained alongside Joseph the duck just in (**19**) _____ anything went wrong and, (**20**) _____ happens with the stars' human counterparts, there is always work for lookalikes.

UNIT 6

Tip of my Tongue

READING

Read this extract from a book about memory and then for questions 1–7, choose the alternative A, B, C or D

THE MAKING OF MEMORY

Memories are our most enduring characteristic. In old age we can remember our childhood eighty or more years ago; a chance remark can conjure up a face, a name, a vision of sea or mountains once seen and apparently long forgotten. Memory defines who we are and shapes how we act more closely than any other aspect of our personhood. All of life is a trajectory from experienced past to unknown future, illuminated only during the always receding instant we call the present, the moment of our actual, conscious experience. Yet our present appears continuous with our past, grows out of **it**, is shaped by it, because of our capacity for memory. It is **this** which prevents the past from being lost, as unknowable as the future. It is memory which thus provides time with its arrow.

For each of us, our memories are unique. You can lose a limb, have plastic surgery, a kidney transplant or a sex-change operation, yet you are still in an important sense recognizably yourself as long as your memories persist. We know who we are, and who other people are, in terms of memory. Lose your memory and you as you, cease to exist, which is why clinical cases of amnesia are so endlessly fascinating and frightening. Advocates of cryonics, that Californian fantasy of quick-freezing the dead until future advances in medical technology can bring **them** back to life, recognize this; **they** propose a computer backup store for the frozen corpse's memories which may somehow be read into the revived body at a future time. But our own human memories are not embedded in a computer, **they** are encoded in the brain, in the ten billion nerve cells that comprise the human cerebrum – and the connections and pathways between these cells. Memories are living processes, which become transformed, imbued with new meanings each time we recall **them**.

Most of us worry that we have a poor memory, that we forget faces, vital appointments. Yet the scale and extent of what any one of us can remember are prodigious. Imagine sitting down and looking at a photograph for a few seconds. Then another, then another... Suppose that a week later I show you the photographs again, each accompanied by a new, different **one**, and ask you to say which you had seen before. How many photographs do you think you could identify correctly before your memory ran out or you became confused? When I asked my colleagues in the lab, their guesses ranged from twenty to fifty. Yet when the experiment is done in reality most people can identify accurately at least *ten thousand* different photographs without showing any signs of 'running out' of memory capacity.

Do we then really forget at all? Are all our past experiences, as some schools of psychoanalysis maintain, encoded in some way within our brains, so that, if only we could find the key to accessing **them**, every detail of our past would become as transparent to us as is the present moment of our consciousness? Or is forgetting functional, so that we record and remember only those things which we have reason to believe are important for our future survival? If **that** were so then to have a perfect memory would not be a help but a hindrance in our day-to-day existence, and the long search for techniques or drugs to improve our memory – a search which goes back far into antiquity – would be at best a chimera.

Above all, how do we remember at all? How can the subtleties of our day-to-day experiences, the joys and humiliations of childhood, the trivia of last night's supper or the random digits of a passing car's number-plate become represented within the mix of molecules, of ions, proteins and lipids that make up the ten billion nerve cells of our brain? It is hard enough to envisage such a great number of cells, it is enough to note that each human brain contains getting on for three times as many nerve cells as there are people alive on the earth today, and that if you were to begin counting the connections between **them** at the rate of one every second, it would take you anything from three to thirty million years to complete your tally. Enough **here** perhaps to store the memories of a lifetime...

And yet there is a problem. During a human lifetime every molecule of our body is replaced many times over, cells die and are replaced, the connections between **them** are made and broken thousands, perhaps millions of times. Yet despite this great flux which constitutes our biological existence, memories remain. No memory within a computer could survive such a complete turnover of all the machine's constituent parts. Somehow just as the shapes of our bodies persist despite the ceaseless ebb and flow of their molecular components, **so do** our memories, embedded in the structure and processes of the brain.

Comprehension

1 Why is memory described as our most enduring characteristic?
   A Old people can remember details of their own childhood.
   B It provides a link between our past and our future.
   C All our actions and behaviour are products of our memory.
   D It is an individual characteristic, unknowable to other people.

2 People are fascinated by cases of amnesia because
   A it is a highly unusual condition.
   B it represents a loss of individual identity.
   C it can be brought on by routine medical treatment.
   D they are afraid that others will not recognize them.

3 What doubts does the author have about cryonics?
   A It oversimplifies the problem.
   B It originated in California.
   C It is completely unscientific.
   D It is too reliant on computers.

4 What is shown by the experiment using photographs?
   A Memory can easily be improved.
   B We worry unnecessarily about our memory.
   C We underestimate our memory.
   D The human memory is very powerful.

5 How might having a perfect memory be a problem?
   A We would confuse present and past.
   B We would remember a lot of irrelevant things.
   C We would need to take drugs to maintain it.
   D We would exhaust the amount of memory available.

6 According to the author, the human brain differs from a computer because of
   A the amount it can store.
   B the speed at which it operates.
   C the range of material it can process.
   D its ability to renew itself.

7 The expressions *flux, ebb and flow* and *turnover* are all used in the final paragraph to describe
   A a rate of change.
   B the consequences of change.
   C a state of change.
   D problems associated with change.

UNIT 6

Vocabulary

Look back at the extract and find words that mean the following. Paragraph numbers are given in brackets and one has been done for you as an example.

    0 an adjective meaning *lasts a long time* (1)   *enduring*
    1 a phrasal verb meaning *to bring to mind* (1)   _____
    2 a noun meaning *a type of line* (1)   _____
    3 a noun meaning *loss of memory* (2)   _____
    4 a noun meaning *people in favour of something* (2)   _____
    5 an adjective meaning *wonderfully large* (3)   _____
    6 a noun meaning *something which gets in the way* (4)   _____
    7 a noun meaning *a fanciful idea* (4)   _____
    8 a noun meaning *events leading to feelings of low-esteem* (5)   _____
    9 a noun meaning *unimportant details* (5)   _____
   10 a verb meaning *imagine* (5)   _____
   11 a noun meaning *a record of a count* (5)   _____
   12 an adjective meaning *deeply buried* (6)   _____

Reference skills

Look at these words which are in **bold** in the extract. In each case say what the word is referring to. One has been done for you as an example.

    0 it (line 12)   =   *our past*   **7** them (line 56)   =   _____
    1 this (line 13)   =   _____   **8** that (line 61)   =   _____
    2 them (line 27)   =   _____   **9** them (line 78)   =   _____
    3 they (line 27)   =   _____   **10** here (line 80)   =   _____
    4 they (line 31)   =   _____   **11** them (line 85)   =   _____
    5 them (line 36)   =   _____   **12** so do (line 92)   =   _____
    6 one (line 43)   =   _____

Wordstress

Underline the stressed syllable on each of these words from the text:

    1 characteristic   **4** accompanied   **7** connection   **10** constituent
    2 illuminated   **5** humiliation   **8** embedded   **11** subtleties
    3 unknowable   **6** appointment   **9** recognisably   **12** components

Prefixes and suffixes

    1 Look at these two words from the extract. Draw lines to show where there are any prefixes and suffixes.
         encoded   *embedded*

    2 Look back at the context in which the words were used. Why has this suffix been used?
         _____

    3 When do prefixes ending in *n* sometimes change to *m*? Can you think of other examples?
         _____

55

UNIT 6

GRAMMAR: Gerund and infinitive

- Some verbs are followed always by a gerund and some always by an infinitive:

  I **enjoy playing** games that involve using my memory.
  I find that I am **unable to remember** numbers very accurately.

- Some verbs can be followed by either a gerund or an infinitive, but the meaning may change:

Try to remember the phone number.	=	Please do it it's important.
Try remembering the phone number.	=	It would be a good idea.
I remembered to post the letter.	=	I didn't forget.
I remember posting the letter.	=	I'm sure I did it.

1 Choose the correct form from the alternatives in brackets in each of these sentences.

1 Are you able (*to memorize/ memorizing*) people's phone numbers?
2 Do you remember (*to go/going*) to the post office last Wednesday?
3 Some people find images easier (*remembering/to remember*) than words.
4 I must remember (*trying/to try*) and phone Phil this evening. I've got a message for him.
5 You can't remember complicated instructions without (*to make/making*) notes.
6 (*To memorize/Memorizing*) data is a learned skill that requires a lot of work.
7 The professor recommends (*using/to use*) nmonics as an aid to memory.
8 Actors say there is no easy way (*to learn/for learning*) their lines.
9 Please don't hesitate (*calling/to call*) me if you need any help.
10 I'm looking forward (*to hear/hearing*) from you in due course.
11 I haven't managed (*to find/finding*) a jacket to match my new pair of trousers.
12 Do you dare (*to ask/asking*) the visiting expert such a leading question?

2 Divide the verbs in the box into two categories:
A – those generally followed by an infinitive and **B** – those generally followed by a gerund.
Some verbs may appear in both categories, depending on their use.

admit	avoid	resist	face	offer	miss
intend	regret	finish	want	risk	mention
forgive	decide	postpone	expect	consider
refuse	hope	learn	plan

A (+infinitive)

_____   _____

_____   _____

_____   _____

_____   _____

_____   _____

B (+ gerund)

_____   _____

_____   _____

_____   _____

_____   _____

_____   _____

_____   _____

56

UNIT 6

PUNCTUATION: Commas and clauses

We often use a comma to separate a clause or an adverb from the main part of the sentence. For sentences **1–10**, put a comma in the correct place and decide which is the clause and which is the subject of the main sentence.

Example: If you press that button the machine will work.
Answer: *If you press that button (clause), the machine (subject) will work.*

1 Before beginning work for the day Tom turned on his computer.

2 First of all I'd like to talk about my own experience.

3 Surprising as it may seem memories are our most enduring characteristics.

4 Apart from Dr Brown nobody knew how to programme the computer.

5 You can borrow my BMW as long as you drive carefully.

6 Far from being cold in the room it turned out to be rather warm.

7 Had it not been for Barbara's help the project would never have been completed.

8 The party will be held in the open air providing that it doesn't rain.

9 Unless you have any objections the meeting will take place on March 4th.

10 Despite the limited time available for rehearsals the band seemed very well prepared.

READING: PRE-READING TASK

1 Look at these three sentences:
   A *The reporter attacked the senator and admitted the error.*
   B *The reporter who attacked the senator admitted the error.*
   C *The reporter who the senator attacked admitted the error.*

   Do all three have the same meaning? Can you explain any differences in meaning?

2 Which of the sentences is the most difficult to understand? Why?

3 Look at the headline of the article. What do you think the article is going to be about?

4 Read the article quickly to decide which of the sentences **A**, **B** or **C**, best summarizes the article.
   A *Scientists prove that the harder the question, the longer the brain takes to answer it.*
   B *Scientists show that the harder a brain works, the more it achieves.*
   C *Scientists find that the more complex the problem, the quicker the brain responds to it.*

57

5 What question did the researchers ask the volunteers? What was the purpose of the question? What other questions do you think they asked?

_____

_____

6 Now read more carefully and then answer the questions which follow.

How grey matter can be red hot

Those irritatingly compulsive teasers which crop up in the back of weekend magazines need never defeat you again. For, according to a fascinating study published recently in *Science*, thinking harder really does make your brain work harder. Researchers in Pittsburg, USA, have concluded that they can measure how hard people are thinking simply by measuring how much brain tissue springs into action. The observations were made using a method that is called 'magnetic resonance imaging'.

Although common sense suggests that the more complex the problem, the harder the brain works, there has always been speculation about whether high levels of cognition can actually be detected in terms of brain activity.

Simply by asking volunteers to look at written sentences, the researchers seemed to have proved that loftier thoughts really are linked to higher brain activity. Their technique may also help scientists to tell exactly which parts of the brain are used to carry out particular mental tasks.

The task chosen for this experiment was understanding written sentences. The researchers chose this because a wide variety of knowledge is required to process the meaning of words, phrases, how they fit together and to develop a visual picture of the meaning.

Fifteen participants of college age were shown the following sentences which increase in complexity:

1 The reporter attacked the senator and admitted the error.
2 The reporter who attacked the senator admitted the error.
3 The reporter who the senator attacked admitted the error.

The ascending order of complexity is confirmed by the fact that the third sentence took the participants longer to read, caused their pupils to dilate more, and was more likely to be misunderstood.

After reading each sentence, they were asked questions such as, 'Did the reporter attack the senator?' They answered by pressing buttons. As this was done, the researchers monitored the brain activity in four areas of the brain known to be associated with language. All areas became more active as the sentences got more complicated, the areas in the left hemisphere of the brain being activated more dramatically. Around three times more brain tissue was used in the left-hand-side areas than in the right hemisphere. The exact amount of brain matter involved varied from person to person and with each set of sentences.

The scientists postulate that the different areas of the brain may have a specific role in deciphering the sentences. Wernicke's area in the left hemisphere may be responsible for processing the meaning of each word and Broca's area, also on the left, may help to associate the sound of the word with its meaning.

The researchers conclude that it is now possible to map how difficult a cognitive task is by looking at how much of the brain is needed to tackle it.

UNIT 6

Language work

1. What do you think 'teasers' (line 2) are? Why does the writer describe them as 'irritatingly compulsive'?

2. Explain in your own words the phrase 'springs into action'. (lines 14–15)

3. What does the writer mean by the term 'common sense'? (line 19)

4. What are 'high levels of cognition'? (lines 24–25)

5. What did the researchers set out to prove?

6. What other theory has been supported by the research?

7. Why did the researchers choose to use written sentences in their research?

8. Explain the phrase 'ascending order of complexity'. (lines 61–62)

9. What three pieces of evidence support the idea that one of the sentences was more difficult to understand?

10. Which side of the brain proved to be the most active? Why?

Grammar: relative pronouns

1. Look again at the three sentences the volunteers were shown. One of them would be much easier to understand had the word *whom* been used instead of *who*. Which sentence is this? When is it possible to use *whom* rather than *who*?

2. In each of the sentences **1–10**, decide which is true, either;
   A *who* can be replaced by *whom*
   or **B** *who* must be replaced by *whom*
   or **C** *who* cannot be replaced by *whom*

   1. John is the man who I go to watch football matches with.
   2. Who is that knocking at the door?
   3. She is the woman who wrote the article about brains.
   4. Rita is the woman with who I had a conversation about the Internet.
   5. 'You are talking about the woman who I love,' he said.
   6. Can you indicate the man to who you sent the letter?
   7. He was the only one of the actors without who the play couldn't go on.
   8. I was wondering who to ask to the party.
   9. Sally is the little girl who we bought the birthday present for.
   10. Who is going to help me do the washing-up this evening?

UNIT 6

3 Add a preposition to these sentences.

Example: This is the person ___for___ whom I've been waiting.

1 Tom is the man _____ whom I bought my old car.
2 Polly is a student _____ whom I communicate on the Internet.
3 What's the name of the person _____ whom you sent that fax?
4 Lizzie is the girl _____ whom we gave our old desktop computer.
5 _____ whom do I have the pleasure of speaking?

Now rewrite each of the sentences above using *who* + preposition as in the example.

Example: *She's the person (who) I've been waiting for.*

6 _____
7 _____
8 _____
9 _____
10 _____

4 Put either *who, whom, where* or *which* into the space in each of these sentences.

Example: James is a man ___who___ likes his food.

1 *Tanamara* is a book _____ I've never read.
2 Frances is the name of the girl _____ I've never met.
3 York is a place _____ I've never visited.
4 Sally is the type of person _____ we ought to employ.
5 Dr Smith is someone _____ you can always rely on.
6 This is the place _____ the accident happened.
7 The company is the only one _____ sells this type of product.
8 This is the only place _____ you can send a fax cheaply.
9 Our problem is finding someone _____ is willing to do this sort of work.
10 Are they made by the company _____ makes the video components?

DISCURSIVE COMPOSITIONS

Write plans for each of these composition titles.

1 'Having a good memory can be both an advantage and a disadvantage in life'. Do you agree? (350 words)
2 'There is no such thing as intelligence; some people can just memorize things much better than others'. Do you think this is true? (350 words)
3 'The ability to forget is sometimes more important than the ability to remember.' In what situations might this be true? (350 words)
4 Describe a childhood experience that you can recall particularly vividly and explain why you think the memory has remained with you so clearly. (350 words)

Now choose the most interesting title and write your composition. Remember to use your plan!

GRAMMAR: Conditional sentences

Remember: There are four main types of conditional sentence:

'zero' | If + present simple + present simple |

If I wake up early, I go for a walk before breakfast. = usually

1st | If + present simple + will + infinitive without *to* |

If I wake up early tomorrow, I will go for a walk before breakfast. = I really will if I have time

2nd | If + subjunctive (past simple) + would + infinitive without *to* |

If I had time, I would go for a walk tomorrow before breafast. = but actually I don't expect to have time
If I were younger, I would go for a walk before breakfast. = but I'm not younger, so I won't

3rd | If + past perfect + would + have + past participle |

If I had woken up earlier, I would have gone for a walk before breakfast. = but I didn't wake up early, so I didn't go

Finish each of the following sentences so that it is **as similar as possible in meaning to the sentence printed before it**.

1. In your place, I would report the incident to the police.
   If _____
2. If you'd taken my advice, you wouldn't be in this mess now.
   Had _____
3. If nobody asks to see your passport, say nothing.
   Unless _____
4. As long as it doesn't rain, the party will be held outdoors.
   Should _____
5. Providing everyone agrees, the meeting planned for next week will be cancelled.
   Unless _____
6. The more practice of driving you get, the more likely you are to pass the test.
   As long _____
7. Let me know if you are ever in need of assistance.
   Should _____
8. Dinner will be served at 8 pm, irrespective of the children's state of readiness.
   Whether _____
9. Unless prices rise dramatically, we'll be able to afford a new car next year.
   Providing _____
10. Regardless of the amount of wind, we'll go sailing tomorrow.
    Whether _____

UNIT 6

SPELLING: Proof reading

It is a good idea to check your written work carefully. Read this passage about phrenology. There is a spelling mistake in each line. Underline each of the mistakes and write the correction in the space on the right.

A quick _surph_ around the internet is enough to confirm that the (0) ____surf____
old art of phrenology is makeing a bit of a comeback. Indeed, (1) _____
our by no means extensive browse reveled more than 600 (2) _____
references to phrenology on the webb. (3) _____
The science of phrenology was developped in Austria in the late 18th (4) _____
century by Franz Joseph Gall, won of the founders of modern neurology. (5) _____
At a time when almost nothing was know about the functioning of the (6) _____
brain, Gall had the amazing insight that diferent regions of the brain (7) _____
might be responsable for different faculties. How well these faculties (8) _____
were developed, acording to Gall, could be judged by feeling the (9) _____
bumps on the relavent part of someone's head. (10) _____

Sadly, phrenology, whilst geting the general idea right, is based on two (11) _____
false premises. Firstly, that the contours of the brian actually follow (12) _____
those of the scull, and secondly that it is possible to equate size with (13) _____
efficiency. Additionaly, Gall got most of his bumps in the wrong places. (14) _____

VOCABULARY: Wordsearch

Find as many words as possible connected with the topic of computers in the grid. Words may run horizontally or vertically. One has been done for you as an example.

C	O	M	P	U	T	E	R	Y	C	D	R	O	M	S
S	I	T	E	D	E	F	A	U	L	T	C	F	D	P
H	R	E	H	I	R	F	M	F	I	F	O	L	A	R
R	F	M	O	O	M	O	O	A	C	I	N	O	T	E
F	L	A	M	E	I	N	D	X	K	L	Y	P	A	A
N	O	I	N	I	N	T	E	R	N	E	T	P	B	D
E	G	L	E	M	A	K	M	D	L	X	C	Y	A	S
W	O	C	T	E	L	E	V	O	A	I	W	D	S	H
B	N	O	W	N	O	Y	T	W	P	T	O	I	E	E
I	M	P	O	U	P	R	I	N	T	E	R	S	W	E
E	O	Y	R	S	A	V	E	L	O	W	D	K	W	T
L	U	R	K	B	B	F	N	O	P	A	S	T	E	E
X	S	J	V	C	O	M	M	A	N	D	W	R	X	D
K	E	Y	B	O	A	R	D	D	R	I	V	E	P	I
W	O	R	D	P	R	O	C	E	S	S	O	R	Q	T

The language of computing is often international. Can you think of other words in English which are connected to the world of computers?

UNIT 7

A Matter of Taste

VOCABULARY: Wordsearch

1 Find as many words as possible connected with the topic of clothing as you can in the grid. Words may run horizontally or vertically. One has been done for you as an example.

```
S  C  A  R  V  E  S  J  A  C  K  E  T  X
E  O  L  L  E  P  L  E  G  G  I  N  G  S
Q  T  Y  Y  S  C  I  A  F  F  B  Y  B  P
U  T  C  C  T  A  P  N  U  U  R  L  A  O
I  O  R  R  O  R  P  S  R  U  O  O  S  L
N  N  A  A  O  D  E  N  I  M  O  N  E  Y
S  H  A  W  L  I  R  S  I  O  C  X  B  E
B  E  L  T  Y  G  S  O  T  V  H  A  A  S
O  S  I  L  K  A  I  C  A  E  B  N  L  T
W  O  O  L  Y  N  O  K  T  R  R  O  L  E
T  R  A  I  N  E  R  S  T  C  A  R  C  R
I  L  E  A  T  H  E  R  O  A  C  A  A  P
E  A  R  R  I  N  G  P  O  O  E  K  P  V
B  O  I  L  E  R  S  U  I  T  S  X  O  C
```

2 Divide the words you have found into three categories:

Articles of clothing	Accessories	Materials
_____	_____	_____
_____	_____	_____
_____	_____	_____
_____	_____	_____
_____	_____	_____
_____	_____	_____
_____	_____	_____
_____	_____	
_____	_____	

3 Which of the words do you associate with:
– good or bad taste?
– style or fashion?

UNIT 7

USE OF ENGLISH: Cloze passage

Fill each of the numbered spaces in the passage with **one** suitable word. One has been done for you as an example.

Scarves as works of art

The scarf is the most versatile and least acclaimed fashion accessory. (**0**) ___The___ simplicity of this square of cloth means that it can be worn in (**1**) _____ manner of ingenious ways, (**2**) _____ fold subtly suggesting the character of the wearer.

The Scarf Show in London is the first exhibition devoted solely (**3**) _____ the scarf. There are over 250 exhibits, many (**4**) _____ private collections, including the bold designer squares some people drape around the neck in (**5**) _____ a way that the label can be seen at every angle.

Wandering through the Scarf Show, (**6**) _____ notices historic changes (**7**) _____ both taste and attitude. The ephemeral 1920s scarves still look elegant, (**8**) _____ the flourescent whirling circles of the 1970s now seem outmoded. However, the prize (**9**) _____ bad taste goes to the 1930s 'fascinator', a creation of black sequins and wiry strings, (**10**) _____ hangs over the head and jingles like a cowbell (**11**) _____ you walk.

Many of the scarves were designed (**12**) _____ well-known fashion designers, whilst others are abstract paintings; (**13**) _____ is work by the artist Patrick Heron, for example, (**14**) _____ loan from the Tate Gallery. The Royal Academy took up the (**15**) _____ of printing pictures from their major exhibitions on to souvenir scarves in the 1980s, and those from their Picasso exhibition, snapped (**16**) _____ by delighted visitors, are now (**17**) _____ collectable.

But perhaps the most valuable item (**18**) _____ all is a scruffy piece of silk which a Second World War airman wore when he was parachuted (**19**) _____ enemy territory. Finely printed on (**20**) _____ sides is an escape map.

Language work

1 Look back at the text. Underline all the adjectives used to talk about the scarves.

2 Divide the adjectives into three groups:

Positive	Negative	Neutral
_____ _____	_____ _____	_____ _____
_____ _____	_____ _____	_____ _____
_____ _____	_____ _____	
_____ _____	_____ _____	
_____		

3 Underline the stressed syllable on each adjective you have found.

4 Make a noun from each of the adjectives and undeline the stressed syllable on the noun.

UNIT 7

GRAMMAR: Gerund versus Infinitive

Put the correct form of the verb in brackets, either gerund or infinitive, in each of the spaces in these sentences.

1. I couldn't resist _____ (go) to see that new exhibition at the National Gallery.
2. Please forgive my _____ (mention) it, but I think you're sitting on my hat.
3. I refuse _____ (accept) the idea of selling that painting, it's been in my family for generations.
4. I've heard that Tom intends _____ (invest) in 1980s furniture which is becoming very collectable.
5. I was completely taken aback _____ (learn) that my old vase was quite valuable.
6. Do you think it's worth _____ (travel) all the way to Paris to see the Cezanne exhibition?
7. What the designer omitted _____ (mention) was the price she wants for the commission.
8. I have arranged for you _____ (borrow) that art book rather than have the expense of buying it.
9. Would you mind _____ (tidy) up your room a bit before you go out, please?
10. I can't face _____ (listen) to another hour of this concert, I'm going home!
11. I can't be bothered _____ (catch) the bus, let's take a taxi.
12. Should you happen _____ (see) Phil, could you tell him I'm looking for him?
13. I'm inclined _____ (agree) with my father, who has no time for Picasso.
14. I resent your _____ (suggest) that my work is not original.
15. Does Molly envisage _____ (visit) the Prado while she's in Madrid?
16. Like many artists, Joshua cannot tolerate people _____ (criticize) his work.
17. Is Gail counting on _____ (get) a grant when she goes to art school?
18. Jason often pretends _____ (be) unemployed, but actually he's a graphic designer.
19. Don't attempt _____ (take) that picture out of its frame, you might damage it.
20. Alison generally appreciates _____ (be) told when her work is not up to standard.

HELP WITH SPELLING 5: Words ending in *cede/ceed/sede*

- There are three ways of spelling words ending with this sound, but most of them are spelled *cede*:
  precede   concede   etc.
- There are four exceptions to this rule which it is worth learning:
  supersede =   the only word where s is used instead of *c*
  exceed, proceed and *succeed* =   the only words which end in *ceed*

Look at these sentences. Each one contains a spelling mistake. The mistake may or may not involve a word ending in *cede/ceed* or *sede*. Underline the misspelled word in each sentence and write a correction in the space on the right.

1. It was a very sucessful concert and all the proceeds went to charity. _____
2. Terry's new novel is not as exciting as the preceeding ones. _____
3. The rock star is now over 50 and his hair is beginning to receed. _____
4. That model of word-processor has now been superceded. _____
5. John conceded that he had made an error of judgment. _____
6. The police officer fined him for exceeding the spede limit. _____
7. Tamsin has succeeded in overcoming many personnal difficulties. _____
8. The lawyer told Ted that legal procedings had been started against him. _____

UNIT 7

USE OF ENGLISH: Structure words

Read this short passage about blue jeans. A number of structure words have been taken out. From the alternatives in brackets, choose the most appropriate word or expression which fits best in the context of the passage.

Blue jeans

Sometime, probably in the sixteenth century, someone invented a tough cotton fabric in the Italian city of Genoa. Which is (**1**) *how/where* we get the word 'jeans' from, (**2**) *or/and* so rumour has it. But the name could have been created (**3**) *also/even* earlier in the French city of Nimes, where it was called 'serge de Nimes', or denim (**4**) *from/for* short. We may not know the origins of the name (**5**) *and/but* what we do know is that this material eventually became a worldwide uniform.

Jeans are the coolest fashion statement there is – (**6**) *unless/providing* you iron in a crease or sport an elasticated waistband, which is when they instantly become the opposite. Alone (**7**) *among/between* cheap, everyday garments, jeans are the only ones that look better (**8**) *as/the* older they get and actually accrue in value (**9**) *with/in* the passage of years.

Jeans have attitude – they say something about you – broadcasting loud (**10**) *and/or* clear that the wearer is proud to be associated (**11**) *to/with* other iconic wearers – (**12**) *such as/as for* James Dean, Bruce Springstein, etc.

Every year millions of pairs are bought all (**13**) *through/over* the world, many of them the classic 501 jean – a style which was first introduced in 1890. In the world of fashion (**14**) *where/whose* things go out of date faster than you can blink, it's (**15**) *almost/hardly* unthinkable for a company to be selling an item designed more than 100 years ago.

WRITING: an article

You have been asked to write a short article of between 150 and 200 words on the subject of blue jeans for an English-speaking magazine read by young people in your country. Look at this brief you have received from the editor:

> *The article should include historical information about denim material, the design of jeans and Levi Strauss himself. You should also include an appraisal of the place of jeans in fashion in your country. I'm enclosing some biodata on Levi Strauss for you to use.*

In your article, use your own words, write in an appropriate style, and include:
- the information from the box below
- ideas from the passage above
- your knowledge about the popularity of jeans in your country

LEVI STRAUSS	
1829	Born in Bavaria, Germany (son of a haberdasher)
1847	Emigrated to New York (where brother had haberdashery business)
1853	Became a US citizen
1853	Moved to San Francisco (time of gold rush)
1872	Went into business with Jacob Davis (Davis had designed the first jeans, but lacked the money to develop the idea)
1902	Died – left fortune of $6 million
1990s	$7 billion worth of jeans sold per year world wide

UNIT 7

VOCABULARY: Prefixes with *up*

Complete each sentence with a word from the box and the prefix *up*. One has been done for you as an example

| ~~bringing~~ hill tight keep shot right turn take set side date |

0   The sculptor's __upbringing__ was very artistic; both her parents were painters.
1   Polly felt very _____ when she heard that her car had been stolen.
2   It's a beautiful old house, but I'm afraid its _____ costs a fortune.
3   Finding the money to put on such a large exhibition was quite an _____ struggle.
4   It's a lovely painting, but I'm afraid it seems to be hanging _____ down.
5   Although the tickets have been on sale for a month, there's been very little _____ so far.
6   Tristan gets very _____ if people keep him waiting.
7   There has been an _____ in the fortunes of female designers in recent years.
8   Sarah will visit us tomorrow to give us an _____ on latest developments in software design.
9   Why is that box lying on its side? I thought it was meant to be kept _____.
10 The _____ of the long discussion about packaging was the decision to employ a new graphic designer.

GRAMMAR: Wishes and regrets

- There are three main uses of the verb *to wish* in the present tense. Compare:

    A *I wish you a happy birthday.*   = the verb followed by an object
    B *I wish you were here (but you're not).*   = the verb followed by the subjunctive
           I wish I could swim (but I can't).
           I wish you would shut up (but you won't).
    C *I wish I hadn't done it (but I did).*   = the verb followed by the past perfect

- The verb *to wish* can also be used in the past tense. Compare:

    A *Sophie wished me a happy birthday.*
    B *Carol wished Paul had been there (but he wasn't).*
           Len wished he could swim (but he couldn't).
           I wished Tom would shut up (but Tom wouldn't).
    C *Sam wished he hadn't lost the money (but he did lose it).*

Rewrite each of the following sentences so that it is **as similar as possible in meaning to the sentence printed before it**, but it uses a form of the verb *to wish*.

1   Terry was disappointed that he couldn't go to the football match.
    Terry wishes _____
2   Sally regrets not sending a postcard to her family when she was on holiday.
    Sally wishes _____
3   Felix phoned Raphaella and said, 'Good luck in your exams tomorrow'.
    Felix phoned to _____
4   Graham found it annoying that he had to visit his grandmother.
    _____
5   Dennis regrets the fact that he isn't better at maths.
    _____

67

UNIT 7

6 Pamela would like to be able to stay out later on Saturday nights.

_____

7 Ronnie would very much like Samantha to help him with his homework.

_____

8 Kelly would be pleased if it stopped raining.

_____

9 Benny would very much like to be able to speak Welsh.

_____

10 Patsy regretted saying that her sister's boyfriend was stupid.

_____

11 I'm sorry that you couldn't come to the party, it was great.

_____

12 It really annoys me the way Racquel keeps leaving that door open.

_____

READING

Read the text carefully and for questions **1–5**, choose the best alternative **A**, **B**, **C** or **D** which fits best.

LETS NOT FIGHT ABOUT IT

I was waiting to go on an American chat show a few years ago for a discussion about how men and women communicate, when a man walked in and politely introduced himself. He told me that he had read and liked my latest book and then added, 'When I get **out there**, I'm going to attack you, but don't take **it** personally. That's why they invited me on this show, so that's what I'm going to do.'

We went on the set and the show began. I had hardly managed to finish a sentence before the man threw his arms out in gestures of anger and began shrieking – briefly hurling accusations at me, and then railing at length about women in general. The strangest thing about his outburst was how the studio audience reacted. They turned vicious – not attacking me or him, but the other guests who came on after us.

My antagonist was nothing more than a dependable provocateur, brought on to ensure a lively show. The incident has stayed with me, however, not because it was typical of the chat shows I have appeared on – it wasn't, I'm glad to say – but because **it** exemplifies the ritual nature of much of the opposition that pervades public dialogue. There is evidence that, in Western culture at least, people prize contentiousness and aggression more than co-operation and conciliation.

It's all part of what I call the argument culture, which rests on the assumption that opposition is the best way to get anything done. The best way to discuss an idea is to set up a debate. The best way to cover news is to find people who express the most extreme of views and present **them** as 'both sides'. The best way to begin an essay is to attack someone. The best way to show you're really thoughtful is to criticize.

I'm not suggesting that passionate opposition and strong verbal attacks are never appropriate. There are moments in life when true invective may be called for. What I'm questioning is the ubiquity, the knee-jerk nature of approaching almost any issue, problem or public person in an adversarial way. Smashing heads does not open minds. Warlike behaviour and language grow out of, but can also lead to, an ethic of aggression. We come to value aggressive tactics for their own sake and compromise becomes a dirty word. We may start to feel guilty if we are conciliatory rather than confrontational, even if we achieve the result we're seeking. This ethic of aggression, what's more, may lead people to take up positions that are more adversarial than they feel, and **this** can then get in the way of reaching a possible solution.

I feel that the roots of this ritualized opposition may lie in the education system in certain countries where a standard way to write an academic paper is to position one's work in opposition to someone else's. **This** creates a need to prove others wrong, which is quite different from reading something with an open mind and discovering that you disagree with it.

And perhaps the most dangerous harvest of this ethic of aggression and ritual fighting is – as with the audience response to the screaming man on the TV show – an atmosphere of animosity that spreads like a fever. In extreme forms, it rears its head in occasional instances of road rage or shooting sprees. In more common forms, it leads to what is decried everywhere as a lack of civility. In other words, it erodes our sense of human connection to those in public life and to the strangers who cross our paths as we lead our daily lives.

Comprehension

1 What did the writer find most surprising about the behaviour of the man on the TV show?
   A That he had read her book.
   B How polite he was beforehand.
   C The effect it had on the audience.
   D What he accused her of.

2 Why does the writer tell us the story about the TV show?
   A She wants to make a point about television.
   B It shows how well people react when challenged.
   C She wants to illustrate certain trends in behaviour.
   D It shows how some situations can be manipulated.

3 According to the writer, people seem to value confrontation more than co-operation because they think it is
   A more effective.
   B more objective.
   C more exciting.
   D more cultured.

4 The writer wants to question people's assumptions about the value of adversarial behaviour because she thinks
   A it may be the result of feelings of guilt.
   B it may make people more selfish.
   C it may stop people tackling some issues.
   D it may not be appropriate to all situations.

5 What does the writer see as the likely long-term consequence of the 'ethic of aggression'?
   A Falling academic standards.
   B A less civilized way of life.
   C Regular acts of senseless violence.
   D Less discussion of important issues.

Language work

1 Which word in paragraph 2 is used to summarize the behaviour of the 'provocateur' on the TV show?

2 Which phrase does the writer use in paragraph 3 to tell us that she has reflected on the chat show experience?

3 In your own words, summarize the point the writer is making through the examples she gives in paragraph 4.

4 Why has the writer put the phrase 'both sides' (line 34) in inverted commas?

5 What synonym of 'strong verbal attacks' does the writer use in paragraph 5?

UNIT 7

6 Which noun, used in paragraph 5, repeats the idea established by the verb 'pervades' in paragraph 3?
_____

7 In your own words, explain what the writer means by the phrase, 'Smashing heads does not open minds' (lines 43–44).
_____

8 What does the writer mean when she says that opposition has become 'ritualized'?
_____

9 What word does the writer use in paragraph 7 to give the idea of 'result'?
_____

Vocabulary

Find these words and phrases in the text. Paragraph numbers are given in brackets and one has been done for you as an example.

0	a superlative meaning *most recent* (1)	*latest*
1	a verb which means *throwing* (2)	_____
2	a verb which means *to place high value on* (3)	_____
3	an adjective which means *automatic and unthinking* (5)	_____
4	a noun which means *a strategy used to get a certain result* (5)	_____
5	a phrase which means *to obstruct* (5)	_____
6	a phrase which means *appears unwelcomely* (7)	_____

Reference skills

Look at these words and phrases which are in **bold** in the text. Say what each word or phrase is referring to. One has been done for you as an example.

0	out there (line 6)	=	*on the set of the TV programme*
1	it (line 7)	=	_____
2	my antagonist (line 18)	=	_____
3	it (line 23)	=	_____
4	it's (line 28)	=	_____
5	them (line 34)	=	_____
6	this (line 52)	=	_____
7	this (line 59)	=	_____
8	others (line 60)	=	_____
9	it (line 67)	=	_____

Summary

In a paragraph of around **75–100 words**, summarize in your own words the reasons why the writer thinks that the confrontational behaviour she describes may be bad for society.

GRAMMAR: Inversions

Finish each of the following sentences so that it is **as similar as possible in meaning to the sentence printed before it.**

1. The car may have been cheap to buy, but it wasn't good value.
   Cheap _____
2. That hotel is elegant, but it lacks the atmosphere of its neighbour.
   Elegant _____
3. Although the painting is pretty, it doesn't compare with the great masters.
   Pretty _____
4. It may seem strange, but Polly has no formal artistic training.
   Strange _____
5. The house, which was built in the eighteenth century, is very well kept.
   Built _____
6. Fred, who actually specializes in making furniture, is also good at painting.
   Also _____
7. Gerry was so engrossed in his novel that he forgot the loaf he'd put in the oven.
   So _____
8. Although I expected her to be late, Daphne arrived at the hotel in good time.
   Contrary _____
9. As I know Gail is a fan of the group, I wasn't surprised to see her at the concert.
   Knowing _____
10. Tony is not in the least bit interested in classical music, he rather likes jazz.
    Far _____
11. Sally's timekeeping was so bad that she risked losing her job.
    So _____
12. William didn't realize he had so much stuff until he had to move house.
    Not until _____

UNIT 8

Go your own Way

USE OF ENGLISH: Cloze passage

Fill each of the numbered spaces in the passage with **one** suitable word. One has been done for you as an example.

Birds of a feather

There is something awe-inspiring (0) __*about*__ large groups of animals – especially when they all move together at the same time. We wonder (1) _____ this unity of purpose comes from, and (2) _____ it is that the individuals know what the group is supposed to do and the part they must (3) _____ in it.

Once, (4) _____ I was visiting friends in Monte Carlo, I witnessed one of the most extraordinary sights I have ever seen. (5) _____ high up in their tower block apartment, I was looking down into the harbour. It was jam-packed (6) _____ expensive yachts, glowing in the light of the setting (7) _____. Way down below me, in among the buildings, was a huge tree – a tree laden _____ (8) with fruit, but with birds. Literally thousands of birds – they (9) _____ like starlings, but I couldn't be sure – were spiralling in to settle (10) _____ for the night.

The sheer concentration of birds was amazing enough, but (11) _____ was more. As the birds dipped and wheeled in the (12) _____, the entire flock began (13) _____ acquire some kind of collective order. At first, it seemed little (14) _____ than a random swarm of independent birds, a scattering of black dots. But as the sun dipped lower, the entire flock began to act as (15) _____, like some gigantic single flying organism. The birds spiralled through the air, swerving and turning with astonishing speed and an inpressive unity as (16) _____ each bird knew exactly (17) _____ to do. Occasionally a large group would (18) _____ off, whirling and swirling in its own independent dance – only to quickly rejoin the main group, as if drawn (19) _____ an invisible magnet.

Then magically, as suddenly as it (20) _____ begun, the flock dispersed, the dance was over.

Vocabulary

1. Look back at the text and find:
   A the adjectives that tell us about how the writer felt
   B the words and phrases that tell us about the number and density of things
   C the nouns and verbs that tell us how things moved

2. Why has the writer chosen to use these words?
   _____

3. Why has he used so many different words?
   _____

Writing: a description

In no more than than 200 words, write a description of a time when you saw something that really impressed you. Before you start:

- think about the event and exactly what happened, where you were, who you were with, etc.
- look back at the cloze passage to see how the writer organized his piece of writing.
- write a list of the words and phrases you could use to describe what you saw.
- think of as many synonyms for the words as you can.

PROVERBS

1 Match the beginning of the common English proverb on the left with the phrase on the right which completes it. One has been done for you as an example.

1	Birds of a feather	A	in one basket.
2	Absence makes	B	laughs longest.
3	Familiarity breeds	C	a book by its cover.
4	Never judge	D	the heart grow fonder.
5	Don't put all your eggs	E	flock together.
6	A bird in the hand	F	but you can't make it drink.
7	While the cat's away	G	is worth two in the bush.
8	You can lead a horse to water	H	before they are hatched.
9	Finders keepers	I	the mice will play.
10	He who laughs last	J	contempt.
11	Don't count your chickens	K	losers weepers.

2 For each of the proverbs above, write a sentence summarizing the idea that it is explaining.

_____
_____
_____
_____
_____
_____
_____
_____
_____
_____
_____

UNIT 8

GRAMMAR: Reporting verbs

Often the meaning of a sentence in direct speech is summarized by a verb in reported speech:
'Would you like to go out for dinner with me, Nigel?' said Fiona.
Fiona invited Nigel out to dinner.

There are three main types of sentence:

- Type A: verb + person + infinitive with 'to'
  The policeman asked Diana to describe the man.

- Type B: verb + infinitive with 'to'
  Gloria agreed to send the company a copy of her CV.

- Type C: verb + -ing
  Alan regretted not studying harder for his exams.
  Tanya apologized for missing the meeting.

N.B. Reporting verbs can often be followed by a clause with *that*, but this is generally avoided unless one of the shorter forms (A–C) would be unclear:
Gloria agreed that she would send the company her CV.
Tanya apologized for the fact that she had missed the meeting.

- Reporting verbs are often also followed by nouns:
  Tanya apologized for her absence from the meeting.

1 Finish each of the following sentences so that it is **as similar as possible in meaning to the sentence printed before it**, but uses the correct form after the reporting verb.

1 'I wish I hadn't eaten so much cake,' said Ricky.
   Ricky regretted _____

2 'I'll send you a postcard as soon as I arrive, Mum,' said Dean.
   Dean promised _____

3 'You're not to go out on your own after dark, Kylie,' said her mother.
   Kylie's mother forbade _____

4 'I think you should try a larger size, Madam,' said the shop assistant.
   The shop assistant advised _____

5 'There's too much noise in this room, I can't concentrate,' said Colin.
   Colin complained _____

6 'Why don't we go home and have a cup of coffee?' suggested Delia.
   Delia suggested _____

7 'Don't forget to take your handkerchief, Mary,' said her grandmother.
   Mary's grandmother reminded _____

8 'I'm afraid I've been lying to you, Pauline,' said John.
   John admitted _____

9 'I'm sorry but I won't take no for an answer, I want to speak to the manager,' said the customer.
   The customer insisted _____

10 'OK, if you insist, I'll take you to the cinema,' said Rachel to her son.
   Rachel agreed _____

UNIT 8

2 For each of the sentences, write a new sentence **as similar as possible in meaning to the original sentence**, but is in indirect speech and uses the word given. This word **must not be altered** in any way.

1 'Hello Tim,' said Lesley, 'I just phoned to say well done for passing your exam.'
congratulate

2 'Would you like me to give you a lift, Linda?' asked Peter.
offered

3 'I did not break that plate!' said Hugh.
denied

4 'I'm afraid the failure of the company was completely my own fault,' said the owner.
blamed

5 'OK, I admit that you have a point there, Gareth,' said Monica.
conceded

6 'Don't on any account touch those dishes, they're very hot,' said Penny to her children.
warned

7 Yes, I realize that I made a serious error of judgement,' said Michaela.
accepted

8 'Why don't you try the restaurant in West Street, Kathy. It's very good,' said Stephen.
recommended

9 'Will you be staying the night with your grandmother, Suzy?' asked her father.
enquired

10 'Go on Paul, try just one mouthful, you might like it!' said Thelma.
urged

SPELLING

Choose the correct spelling of each word **A**, **B**, **C**, or **D** to complete each of the sentences **1–10**.

1 Harry _____ in taking a photograph of the wonderful birds.
  A succeeded   **B** suceeded   **C** succeded   **D** sucseeded

2 This drawer is a mess, I really need to _____ it out.
  A sought   **B** saught   **C** sorte   **D** sort

3 Although I spend a lot of time alone, I rarely suffer from _____.
  A lonliness   **B** lonelyness   **C** loneliness   **D** lonlieness

UNIT 8

4 Tony _____ greatly from the work experience scheme he took part in.
  A benefitted   B benafitted   C bennefited   D benefited

5 After the long race, Trixie was _____ tired.
  A noticably   B noticeabally   C noticeably   D noticabley

6 The general feeling was that further investment in the project was _____.
  A unecessary   B unneccessary   C unnecessary   D unneccesary

7 _____, they arrived too late to see the beginning of the play.
  A Unfortunately   B Unfortuneately   C Unfortunateley   D Unfortunatley

8 The animal sanctuary is a place of great _____.
  A tranquility   B tranqillitty   C tranqiulity   D tranquillity

9 The apostrophe is often used to indicate _____.
  A possesion   B possecion   C possession   D posession

10 After the formal dinner, the headmaster _____ to make a long boring speech.
  A preceeded   B proceded   C preseded   D proceeded

READING

This is an extract from a famous detective novel by Dorothy L. Sayers. The detective Peter Wimsey, is having dinner with a group of female academics in an Oxford college in the 1930s. Read the extract and answer the questions which follow.

Gaudy night

'The book,' said the Dean, 'is about a young man who starts out to be a scientist and gets on very well until, just as he's going to be appointed to an important executive post, he finds he's made a careless error in a scientific paper. He didn't check his assistant's results or something. Somebody finds out, and he doesn't get the
5 job. So he decides he doesn't really care about science after all.'
   'Obviously not,' said Miss Edwards. 'He only cared about the post.'
   'But,' said Miss Chilperic, 'If it was only a mistake...'
   'The point about it,' said Peter, 'is what an elderly scientist says to him. He tells him: "the only ethical principle which has made science possible is that the truth shall be told
10 all the time. If we do not penalize false statements made in error, we open up the way for false statements by intention. And a false statement of fact, made deliberately, is the most serious crime a scientist can commit." Words to that effect. I may not be quoting quite correctly.'
   'Well, that's true, of course. Nothing could possibly excuse falsification.'
15 'There's no sense in deliberate falsification, anyhow,' said the Bursar. 'What could anybody gain by it?'
   'It has been done,' said Miss Hillyard, 'frequently. To get the better of an argument. Or out of ambition.'
   'Ambition to be what?' cried Miss Lydgate. 'What satisfaction could one possibly get
20 out of a reputation one knew one didn't deserve? It would be horrible.'
   Her innocent indignation upset everyone's gravity.
   'How about the Forged Decretals... Chatterton... Ossian.... Henry Ireland... those Nineteenth century pamphlets the other day...'
   'I know,' said Miss Lydgate, perplexed. 'I know people do it. But why? They must be
25 mad.'

'In the same novel,' said the Dean, 'somebody deliberately falsifies a result – later on, I mean – in order to get a job. And the young scientist who made the original mistake finds it out. But he says nothing, because the other man is very badly off and has a wife and family to keep.'

'Those wives and families!' said Peter.

'Does the author approve?' inquired the Warden.

'Well,' said the Dean, 'the book ends there, so I suppose he does.'

'But does anybody approve? A false statement is published and the man who could correct it lets it go, out of charitable consideration. Would anybody here do that? There's your test case, Miss Barton, with no personalities attached.'

'Of course one couldn't do that,' said Miss Barton. 'Not for ten wives and fifty children.'

'It sounds anyway, like a manufactured case,' said Miss Allison briskly. 'It could seldom happen and if it did…'

'Oh it happens,' said Miss de Vine. 'It has happened. It happened to me. I don't mind telling you – without names, of course. When I was at Flamborough College, there was a professor who sent in a very interesting thesis on a historical subject. It was a most persuasive piece of argument; only I happened to know that the whole contention was quite untrue, because a letter that absolutely contradicted it was actually in existence in a certain very obscure library in a foreign town. I'd come across it when I was reading up something else. That wouldn't have mattered, of course. But the internal evidence showed that the man must have had access to that library. So I had to make an enquiry, and I found that he really had been there and must have seen the letter and deliberately suppressed it.'

'But how could you be so sure he had seen the letter?' asked Miss Lydgate anxiously. 'He might carelessly have overlooked it. That would be a very different matter.'

'He had not only seen it,' replied Miss De Vine; 'He stole it. We made him admit as much. He had come upon that letter when his thesis was nearly complete, and he had no time to rewrite it. And it was a great blow to him apart from that, because he had grown very enamoured of his own theory and couldn't bear to give it up.'

'That's a mark of an unsound scholar, I'm afraid,' said Miss Lydgate in a mournful tone.

'But there is one curious thing,' went on Miss de Vine. 'He was unscrupulous enough to let the false contention stand; but he was too good a historian to destroy the letter. He kept it.'

'You'd think,' said Miss Pyke, 'it would be as painful as biting on a sore tooth.'

'Perhaps he had some idea of rediscovering it some day,' said Miss de Vine, 'and setting himself right with his conscience. I don't know, and I don't think he knew very well himself.'

'What happened to him?' asked Harriet.

'Well, that was the end of him, of course. He lost the professorship, naturally, and they took away his MA degree as well. A pity, because he was brilliant in his own way – and very good looking, if that has anything to do with it.'

'Poor man!' said Miss Lydgate. 'He must have needed the post very badly.'

'It meant a good deal to him financially. He was married and not well off. I don't know what became of him. That was about six years ago. He dropped out completely. One was sorry about it, but there it was.'

'You couldn't possibly have done anything else,' said Miss Edwards.

'Of course not. A man as undependable as that is not only useless, but dangerous. He might do anything.'

'You'd think it would be a lesson to him,' said Miss Hillyard. 'It didn't pay, did it? Say he sacrificed his professional honour for the women and children that we hear so much about – but in the end it left him worse off.'

'But that,' said Peter, 'was only because he committed the extra sin of being found out.'

UNIT 8

Comprehension

1. In the book, the young scientist failed to get the job because of his lack of
   A honesty.
   B thoroughness.
   C interest.
   D commitment.

2. In the book, the elderly scientist felt that the young scientist
   A had been treated unfairly.
   B was unlucky to have been detected.
   C deserved to lose the job.
   D had intended to deceive people.

3. The Dean suggests that the young scientist's actions at the end of the book show him to be
   A totally unreliable.
   B bitter and disillusioned.
   C completely innocent.
   D very compassionate.

4. What did Miss de Vine's enquiry to the library show?
   A The letter had been stolen.
   B The professor had seen the letter.
   C The professor had visited the library.
   D The letter had been damaged.

5. What interpretation does Miss de Vine put upon the professor's actions regarding the letter?
   A He hadn't understood its significance.
   B He knew it would be discovered eventually.
   C He was inadequate as a historian.
   D He wanted the truth to be preserved.

6. What does Peter suggest about academic life in his final comment?
   A Falsification is always wrong.
   B Falsification may be quite common.
   C The professor was used as a scapegoat.
   D The professor was hypocritical.

Language work

1. In your own words, explain why the elderly scientist felt that all errors had to be penalized.

2. In your own words, explain what an 'ethical principle' is. (line 9)

3. What does Peter mean by the phrase 'words to that effect'. (line 12)

4. In your own words, explain what Miss Hillyard means by 'to get the better of an argument'? (line 17)

5. In what sense is Miss Lydgate's indignation 'innocent'? (line 21)

6 What are the 'forged decretals' an example of? (line 22)

7 In your own words, explain what the phrase, 'let it go' means. (line 34)

8 What conclusions does the Dean draw from the way in which the book ends?

9 What does Miss Barton mean by the phrase 'no personalities attached'? (line 35)

10 What does Miss Allison mean by the phrase 'a manufactured case'? (line 38)

11 Which phrasal verb tells us about the circumstances under which Miss de Vine originally found the letter?

12 Compare the meaning of the word 'happened' in lines 40 and 43.

13 Which word in the second half of the extract tells us about the professor's attitude to his theory?

14 In your own words, explain how and why the professor might have 'rediscovered' the letter. (line 61)

15 What do you understand by the phrase 'he dropped out completely'? (line 70)

16 What does Miss Hillyard mean by the phrase 'it didn't pay'. (line 75)

Summary

In a paragraph of around **100 words**, describe in your own words what happened to the professor Miss de Vine tells the group about. Be sure to mention:
– what he did
– why it was wrong
– how he was discovered
– what happened as a result

Wordstress

Underline the stressed syllable on each of these words from the text.

1	executive	6	persuasive	11	indignation	16	correctly
2	falsification	7	ethical	12	contradicted	17	personalities
3	manufactured	8	reputation	13	deliberately	18	unscrupulous
4	obviously	9	contention	14	considerations	19	charitable
5	satisfaction	10	penalize	15	enamoured	20	professorship

UNIT 8

USE OF ENGLISH: Gap-fill sentences

1 For questions 1–18, complete the sentences with a phrase from the box. One has been done for you as an example.

> a far cry   a lot to be   as far as   as long as   be it from me   better than   burst its   cat amongst
> couldn't care   grown accustomed to   help thinking   her socks   ~~like hot~~
> on behalf of   once and for   rid of   stand much chance   stand on   use your trying

0 These new scarves have been selling _____*like hot*_____ cakes recently.
1 Since her marriage to the boss, Brenda has _____ a much higher standard of living.
2 If Debbie doesn't pull _____ up, she risks losing her job.
3 It's time you got _____ that old coat, it's completely worn out.
4 You've really put the _____ the pigeons by telling Phil what Jenny said.
5 You can borrow my laptop computer _____ don't break it.
6 It's no _____ to hide the pieces, she'll know that it's missing.
7 I can't _____ that Lily wasn't telling the whole truth, you know.
8 Don't _____ ceremony, help yourselves to more cake if you want.
9 Ed's certainly bright, but I wouldn't go _____ to say he's a genius.
10 I know you worry about the environment, but I'm afraid most people _____ less.
11 His large new house is _____ from the small cottage he used to live in.
12 The correctness of your spelling leaves _____ desired, I'm afraid.
13 I want to see this dispute settled for _____ all.
14 Far _____ to accuse your son of stealing, Mrs Smith.
15 I would like to wish you every happiness _____ all the staff at Johnson's.
16 The river _____ banks and nearby fields were flooded.
17 You should have known _____ to hurt her feelings with a comment like that.
18 Unfortunately, Des doesn't _____ of getting a promotion this year.

2 Complete each of the blanks in these sentences with a suitable word or phrase.

1 During the night, group members _____ in turns to stay awake and guard the gear.
2 Don't breathe _____ to anyone about this, it's a secret.
3 Seeing those pictures on the TV news really _____ home to me how terrible it must be to live near a volcano.
4 I really get very fed _____ all this cold damp weather.
5 The staff car park is strictly _____ bounds to students who have no business being there.
6 Where's Toby? It's not like _____ miss a party.
7 Little _____ expect to meet my neighbour when on holiday in the USA.
8 I'm afraid the hotel failed to live _____ the claims made for it in the brochure.
9 Hardly a day passes _____ item of junk mail coming through my letterbox.
10 Nothing I'd read in the guidebooks _____ for the beauty of the valley which now lay before me.

UNIT 9

Nose to the Grindstone

VOCABULARY: Wordsearch

1 Find as many words as possible connected with the world of work in the grid. Words may run horizontally or vertically. One has been done for you as an example.

```
E  M  P  L  O  Y  E  E  S  T  A  F  F  Q
C  A  R  I  N  G  F  I  R  M  O  A  A  U
O  N  O  X  B  O  F  F  I  C  E  X  C  A
M  A  F  P  U  E  I  R  T  O  W  W  T  L
P  G  I  E  S  A  C  A  R  M  A  O  O  I
A  E  T  R  I  R  I  U  A  P  G  R  R  F
N  M  A  S  N  N  E  D  I  E  E  K  Y  I
Y  E  B  O  E  I  N  O  N  T  S  L  R  C
X  N  L  N  S  N  T  P  I  I  G  O  R  A
J  T  E  N  S  G  C  O  N  T  R  A  C  T
O  O  P  E  R  S  S  S  G  O  F  D  D  I
B  S  A  L  A  R  Y  T  O  R  G  A  S  O
R  E  F  E  R  E  N  C  E  P  E  R  K  N
R  E  D  U  N  D  A  N  C  Y  B  O  S  S
```

2 Divide the words you have found into these two categories:

Nouns	(adjectives)			Adjectives	(nouns)
_____	_____	_____	_____	_____	_____
_____	_____	_____	_____	_____	_____
_____	_____	_____	_____	_____	_____
_____	_____	_____	_____		
_____	_____	_____	_____		
_____	_____	_____	_____		
_____	_____	_____	_____		
_____	_____	_____	_____		
_____	_____	_____	_____		
_____	_____	_____	_____		
_____	_____	_____	_____		

3 Form adjectives out of the nouns and nouns out of the adjectives.

4 Underline the stressed syllable on each of the words you have found.

81

UNIT 9

READING: Pre-reading task

1. You are going to read an article about somebody who has a very specialized job. Look at the first paragraph of the article and find the person's:
   - job title
   - special area of interest

2. Read the whole article quickly and decide which heading from the box below best summarizes the topic of each paragraph.

> types of headache   symptoms of headaches   recent research into headaches   causes of headaches
> cure for headaches   headache sufferers   remedies for headaches   theories about headaches
> Marcia Wilkinson's background   prospects for the future

3. Now read the article more carefully and answer the questions which follow.

MOTHER OF HEADACHES

The British neurologist, Marcia Wilkinson, known to colleagues as Mother Migraine, has been studying headaches since 1953. She recognizes 149 causes of headaches and probably knows more about the subject than anyone else in the galaxy. Recently, Dr Wilkinson was the star at the European Headache Federation where she wowed the 783 delegates with her lecture on 'Great Names in Headache History' – the great names being people who had investigated headaches rather than sufferers.

One in ten people in Britain suffer from migraine, 30% get headaches and 98% of everyone in the world gets a headache on occasion. The occasion, says Dr Wilkinson, may be when you are hit on the head with a hammer. As children, boys are more likely to suffer. After the onset of puberty, women suffer three times as often as men. When it comes to migraine, most sufferers are struck by the time they are twenty years old and it is rare to get it for the first time after the age of fifty. As pharmaceutical companies never tire of telling us, 50 million work days a year are lost in headaches, at some cost to business. This figure was somewhat inflated by Alan Frost, a computer engineer, who was dismissed in 1993 after taking off 175 days in two years with a cold and headache.

There are different kinds of headache – the everyday tension headache, the more selective migraine and, mother of all headaches, the cluster headache. A headache, says Dr Wilkinson, is really just a pain in the face; it may occur 15–20 times a month. Migraine is an episodic headache which lasts from four to 72 hours, comes up to four times a month, is associated with vomiting and nausea and is sometimes preceded by flashing lights. The cluster headache comes in bouts lasting 4–6 weeks, with up to 20 attacks per day.

The geography of the headache is important to the diagnosis – whether it is in the front of the head, ventures further afield to the top of the head or takes a trip to the back of the head. Patients variously describe symptoms as being like an iron in the temple, a hot poker behind the eyes, a hammer in the skull or a tight band around the head. Sufferers describe everything from blind spots, zigzag lines and flashing lights to Catherine wheels in front of their eyes.

There are, says Dr Wilkinson, almost as many triggers to headaches as there are people having them. There is the 'salami' headache, triggered by nitrates in the meat. The 'cappuccino' headache, courtesy of caffeine. The 'perfume' headache, sparked off by strong smells. Plus those brought on by coughing, laughing, flashing lights, too many painkillers, loud noise, lack of food, taking holidays, not taking holidays, too much exertion, too much sleep, onions, ice-cream, citrus fruits, chocolate and Chinese takeaways.

There are no end of different theories about headaches. The Ancient Egyptians apparently blamed the ache on evil spirits and went in for a bit of trepanning – drilling a hole in the head to let the spirits out. 'Did that work?' I asked doubtfully. 'I think, if the patient survived, it probably did. You know, the greater pain removing the lesser,' replied Dr Wilkinson with a smile. In the 11th century, doctors stitched a clove of garlic into the temple, in an attempt to relieve headache pain (my question answered as above). By the 17th century, the Swiss were shaving heads and covering them with poisonous flies whose bites were supposed to alleviate headache. 'Counter irritation,' explains Dr Wilkinson. Until late Victorian times, Europeans pulled out teeth to make headaches disappear (answer as above). Less extreme sufferers would follow peculiar diets, like not eating anything except stewed lamb and pears. Did that work? 'If you believe in things,' says Dr Wilkinson, 'they work.'

Scientists become like headless chickens when it comes to headaches. Like the common cold, this is a little-understood area. You can read the works of Wolff, the seminal headache author; dip into the headache classifications of Dr Arnold Friedman; investigate the 5–0HT theory of chemical disturbance; or subscribe to the German neurologist Hartwig Heyck's analysis. Unlike me, Dr Wilkinson understands these. But nothing is proven. 'Nobody,' she says, 'actually knows why a headache comes on'.

Worse still, says Dr Wilkinson, there's no cure. Yes, you can take the new wonder drug Sumatripan, or pick some feverfew, the herb that is traditionally thought good for headaches, or take aspirin. But these only alleviate the symptoms. Dr Wilkinson breaks into rhyme; 'They murmured as they took their fees; there is no cure for this disease'. She says, 'That should be stuck up in every physician's consulting room.'

Whatever the cause, the headache has been bewildering scientists for ages. This is because headaches unlike, say, blood pressure, are hard to measure. Patients can come up with horrid descriptions of their aches, but relatively little money and time have been dedicated to research as it is notoriously difficult to do research on sufferers. If someone tells you he always gets headaches on Tuesdays, it is absolutely certain that once you've got him into hospital on a Tuesday, he won't have a headache. Virtually nobody has a headache in hospital. 'Most of the research,' adds Dr Wilkinson gloomily, 'has been done on chronic medical misuse (caused by too many drugs) and tension headaches'.

The question exercising scientists today is whether animals get headaches. There seems not much point in trying headache medicines on them if they don't have headaches in the first place. One doctor took photographs of monkeys in Australia which looked, with their furrowed brows and forehead-rubbing paws, as though they were suffering from a headache. But, of course, there's no saying whether they do have headaches or not. The last word goes to Dr Wilkinson, she's been suffering from headaches for 72 years and if she can't get rid of them, probably nobody can.

Comprehension

1. Statistics show that your chances of becoming a migraine sufferer
   - A increase as you get older.
   - B are greater when you are young.
   - C increase once you have begun work.
   - D are higher if you live in Britain.

2. According to the article, the most severe form of headache occurs
   - A quite regularly each month.
   - B in combination with other symptoms.
   - C as a result of tension in the face.
   - D over fairly lengthy periods of time.

3. The word 'triggers' (line 46) is used to refer to
   - A symptoms of headaches.
   - B treatments of headaches.
   - C causes of headaches.
   - D results of headaches.

4. How does Dr Wilkinson regard ancient remedies for headaches?
   - A With indifference.
   - B With scepticism.
   - C With disbelief.
   - D With respect.

UNIT 9

5 What does Dr. Wilkinson see as the main problem in studying headaches?

- **A** There is insufficient scientific data.
- **B** Scientific theories have been disproved.
- **C** Traditional remedies seem to be best.
- **D** Doctors do not take the problem seriously.

6 Why may new headache cures not prove particularly effective?

- **A** Animals respond badly to them.
- **B** They seem actually to cause headaches.
- **C** There is no good way to trial them.
- **D** Dr Wilkinson has tried them without success.

Language work

1 In your own words, explain who the 'Great Names in Headache History' were. (line 8)

2 In your own words, explain what is meant by the phrase 'the figure was somewhat inflated'. (lines 22–23)

3 Which two expressions are used to describe movement in paragraph 4?

4 Which words in paragraph 5 echo the verb 'to trigger' as used in line 48?

5 Which phrase in paragraph 6 is used to mean 'without number'?

6 Explain in your own words, why the writer describes the scientists as 'headless chickens'. (line 75)

7 Which word, used in paragraph 9, sums up the state of scientific research into headaches?

8 Which phrase in the last paragraph is used to describe a situation where there is inconclusive evidence of something?

9 What idea of the character of Dr Wilkinson do we get from the article? Underline some words and phrases that give us this idea.

10 What do you think of the style in which the article is written? Find some examples of words and phrases that illustrate this.

11 To what extent do you think the article is:

educational?   scientific?   entertaining?   objective?   informative?

12 What type of reader do you think the article was intended for?

Writing: an article and a speech

Marcia Wilkinson is coming to give a talk entitled 'The History of Headaches' at a college in your town. You have been asked to write two short paragraphs of about 100 words in length.

1. A short informal article for a local English language magazine for students. The aim of the article is to encourage students to come and hear Dr Wilkinson talk by:
    - giving them an idea of the sort of person she is
    - explaining what she will be talking about

2. A short formal speech to be read out as an introduction to Dr Wilkinson's talk. In the speech you should:
    - welcome her
    - tell the audience something about her background
    - introduce the topic of her talk

GRAMMAR: Conversational devices using auxiliary verbs

1 Question tags

- A question tag is a short interrogative phrase added to the end of a statement:
  it's a lovely day, isn't it?
  statement   tag

- Negative tags are added to positive statements and positive tags are added to negative statements.
  It's a lovely day, isn't it?   *It isn't such a nice day today, is it?*
  statement (+) tag (−)   statement (−)   tag (+)

N.B. Imperative statements take a positive tag, unless qualified with *please* or *do*:
  *Sit down, **will** you?*
  ***Please** take a seat, **won't** you?*
  ***Do** shut that door, **won't** you?*

- The question tag repeats the auxiliary verb used in the statement, and the subject pronoun. If there is no auxiliary verb in the statement, *do* is used:
  *You **can** swim, **can't** you?*   *You like rock music, **don't** you?*

- Question tags are commonly used in conversation in one of two ways:

  With rising intonation as an alternative way of asking a question. In this case a reply is expected:

  I think you're Mr Smith, aren't you?

  With falling intonation as a rhetorical question that requires no direct answer:

  The weather is really hot, isn't it?

Add a question tag to the main part of each of these statements.

1. Manchester United played well last night, _____?
2. Rosy really loves going dancing, _____?
3. They're not so keen on strong coffee in the USA, _____?
4. You will come to the party on Saturday, _____?
5. The boys must have got home very late last night, _____?
6. I'd better go and buy a newspaper, _____?
7. Carol made such a fuss about that broken vase, _____?
8. You would like to come to the cinema, _____?
9. You had a nice time at the theatre, _____?

UNIT 9

10 Harry hadn't met Barbara before, _____?
11 It used to be a lot tidier in the city centre, _____?
12 You should've aimed to arrive earlier, _____?
13 We don't need to show our passports at the border, _____?
14 She'd rather book my train ticket in advance, _____?
15 The family usually has dinner at around 7 pm, _____?
16 Let's go out for a drive in the car, _____?
17 You will come and visit me in London, _____?
18 I'm afraid I've made a mistake, _____?
19 I think it's getting rather late for afternoon tea, _____?
20 Let me help you with those bags, _____?

2 So/nor/neither

These words are used with auxiliary verbs as a quick way of expressing agreement.

- Use *so* to agree with a positive statement:
  'I'm really tired.'   'So am I.'

- If there is no auxiliary verb in the statement, *do* is used:
  'I like Greek food.'   'So do I.'

- Use *neither* or *nor* to agree with a negative statement:
  'I can't see that street on the map.'   'Nor can I.' or 'Neither can I.'

Complete the gaps in these responses to statements to produce agreement using *so/nor/neither*.

1 'Peter likes football.'   '_____ Helen.'
2 'My sister will be disappointed.'   '_____ my brother.'
3 'I'd rather play tennis than badminton.'   '_____ I.'
4 'We are not keen on horror films.'   '_____ we.'
5 'My country is warmer than Antarctica.'   '_____ mine.'
6 'I've never seen so many wasps as today.'   '_____ I.'
7 'I usually have dinner late at night.'   '_____ my brother.'
8 'My car doesn't have a sun roof.'   '_____ my father's.'
9 'My French is not very good.'   '_____ your English.'
10 'I used to play the guitar at school.'   '_____ I.'
11 'We'd better be going now.'   '_____ I.'
12 'Tim's never been to Las Vegas.'   '_____ Molly.'
13 'Rita might be late this evening.'   '_____ Pete.'
14 'I can't believe it's time to go already.'   '_____ I.'
15 'I mustn't forget to go to the bank.'   '_____ I.'
16 'Sally oughtn't to walk home alone.'   '_____ Liz.'
17 'My car's not cleaned very often.'   '_____ mine.'
18 'Julie may not be ready on time.'   '_____ Gracie.'
19 'Saturday's not a good day to go fishing.'   '_____ Sunday.'
20 'I'd had to leave my car at home that day.'   '_____ I.'

3 Predicative so/not

- Look at these examples:
  'Do you think it's going to rain?'   'I think so.'
                                         'I don't think so.'
                                           'I think not.'

How many of the words and phrases in the box can be used instead of *think* in each of the example replies above?

| believe | wonder | like | understand | appreciate | I'm afraid | hope | realize | suppose | guess |
| decide | trust | doubt | reckon | presume | report | I'm surprised | wish | rather | remember |

SPELLING: Commonly misspelled words

1 Each of the following words has a letter missing. Mark the word like the example to show where the extra letter should go, and write the letter in the space provided.

Example: a|cidentally   _c_

1 accomodation __
2 exagerate __
3 litrature __
4 businesman __
5 facinate __
6 disapearance __
7 goverment __
8 disapointed __
9 imediately __
10 embarrased __
11 nowledge __
12 necesity __
13 oportunity __
14 recomend __
15 transfered __

2 Each of the following words has an extra letter which is not needed. Cross out the extra letter in each one.

Example: dis~~s~~appointed

1 arguement
2 auxilliary
3 begginning
4 develope
5 equippment
6 labouratory
7 neccessary
8 occassionally
9 ommitted
10 parallell
11 personnell
12 preceede
13 pronounciation
14 responsiability
15 strenghth
16 successfull
17 marketting
18 grammattical

GRAMMAR: Inversion

Finish each of these sentences so that it is **as similar as possible in meaning to the sentence printed before it**.

1 When Ken put the phone down, it immediately started ringing again.
   No sooner _____

2 Robert has never, on any occasion, gone against his father's wishes.
   On no _____

3 My fiancée and I phone each other almost every day.
   Hardly _____

4 Every single plant in the garden was killed by the heavy frost.
   Not a _____

5 Without Yvonne's expert advice, the wedding dress would never have been finished in time.
   Only thanks _____

UNIT 9

6 The Browns finally managed to buy their own flat after years of saving up.
Only _____

7 Tom's lottery winnings were substantial, but not enough to pay off his debts.
Substantial _____

8 I really didn't expect to see Antonietta at Malcom's party.
Little _____

9 Ted hated his father so much that he didn't even visit him on his 90th birthday.
So great _____

10 Pete had forgotten about his promise to his family until one day he got a letter from his sister.
It wasn't _____

USE OF ENGLISH: Cloze passage

Fill each of the numbered spaces in the passage with **one** suitable word.

Desktop publishing

With just a computer, appropriate software and a printer, anyone can (**1**) _____ a home-based publisher. All you need, (**2**) _____ from the equipment, is a good idea.

Take the example of Janice West, a former teacher from Newcastle, who saw a gap (**3**) _____ the market for a free newsletter for local parents telling (**4**) _____ about children's events in the area. Janice had (**5**) _____ up teaching after her third child was born. As a mother at home with young children, Janice realized that it wasn't easy getting out (**6**) _____ about with them and what was needed was a guide (**7**) _____ local child-friendly events.

(**8**) _____ started was fairly straightforward. Janice had an acorn computer, a simple publishing software package and she made a deal (**9**) _____ a local printer who agreed to run (**10**) _____ five thousand copies of her new publication (**11**) _____ she called *Kids Direct*.

Janice distributed the free magazine through nurseries, libraries, schools and playgroups. She also got in (**12**) _____ with private schools and local companies providing services for children to see (**13**) _____ they wanted to advertise. It was the income from this advertising that paid for the production of the magazine and (**14**) _____ Janice with a source of income.

The magazine now (**15**) _____ out once a school term and each issue (**16**) _____ Janice about sixty hours to produce. Although demand for the magazine was high from (**17**) _____ outset, Janice had to work hard to build (**18**) _____ her advertising revenue. Now the magazine (**19**) _____ her in around £10,000 a year net profit and she has recently (**20**) _____ on a deputy to split the workload with her. She is now working on a new magazine to be published in other local areas.

Writing: a formal letter

You are interested in setting up a magazine in your home area and decide to write to Janice to ask for her advice. In a letter of about 150 words:
  – introduce yourself
  – describe your home area
  – describe your idea
  – ask Janice some questions

UNIT 10

The Road Ahead

VOCABULARY: Multiple choice

In this section, you must choose the word, **A**, **B**, **C** or **D** which best completes each sentence.

1. Most fathers were _____ pressure at work and so had little time for the children.
   A under   **B** with   **C** among   **D** against

2. Ten per cent of insurance claims _____ out to be unfounded.
   A come   **B** end   **C** turn   **D** find

3. Services were disrupted during a long _____ of bad weather.
   A stretch   **B** shower   **C** spell   **D** series

4. The local council decided to _____ a policy of zero tolerance towards gutter punks.
   A agree   **B** assert   **C** attend   **D** adopt

5. The programme will go _____ as one of the greatest in TV history.
   A through   **B** along   **C** around   **D** down

6. My son Jason is always _____ my attention.
   A calling   **B** asking   **C** forcing   **D** demanding

7. My golden rule is not to _____ aspersions on how other people bring up their children.
   A make   **B** give   **C** cast   **D** waste

8. The child's temperament seemed to _____ little relation to that of its parents.
   A hold   **B** bear   **C** include   **D** keep

9. Most companies seem able to _____ the worst effects of downsizing from emerging.
   A prevent   **B** persuade   **C** avoid   **D** divert

10. That woman sees nothing _____ in letting her children run around as they wish.
    A awry   **B** amiss   **C** afraid   **D** alike

READING

Read this article from a holiday magazine and answer the questions which follow.

On Four Legs you can take forever

There is no doubt about it, there can be few better countries to explore by road than Ireland. Many of the roads are wide, the traffic light, and governed for the most part by a courtesy long forgotten throughout the rest of Europe. But the slower you go, the more you can enjoy Ireland, so the obvious choice is to swap four wheels for four legs. I decided to hire a horse caravan to take me from site to site and the gaily-painted red and yellow vehicle became my home for a week; transport and company provided by a Grey called Born.

It was a strange sensation to be a holiday-maker and yet become part of the tourist landscape with cameras pointed at me at all times of the day. Coaches full of flashing lenses passed slowly, occasionally frightening the horse to a stand-still. Several inquisitive drivers also asked to look inside. What they saw may have put them off. These wagons are a long way from the comforts of the modern caravan. They are cosy for one, but can supposedly be occupied by up to five. Bedding, pots and pans, knives and forks, and a bottle-gas cooker are the only concessions to modernity.

When you begin one of these trips, you spend the first night in the stable yard getting used to the caravan. School starts at 9.30 in the morning. The mysteries of bridles, bits, collars and other paraphernalia are explained to the uninitiated and a few basic rules are outlined. Like the fact that the horses will always try to take the shortest arc round a corner, something a wheeled vehicle will not do. They then sell you some insurance in case you leave half the caravan behind in your hurry to get out of the campsite. And so to the road.

You do not really need any equestrian experience, the horses are, for the most part, quiet and compliant animals and you soon get into a routine: get up, go to field, run round field hopefully waving a carrot, and then watch while some know-it-all collects your horse with a few quiet words. After feeding and brushing the horse, you put on its bridle and all the other strange bits of kit, and set off, usually stopping the caravan half a mile down the road to run back and collect all the stuff that's fallen out of the cupboard which you forgot to close. You then travel eight to ten miles with horse and caravan, finally arriving at a campsite, where you feed, water and brush the horse again before putting it in a field until tomorrow.

If you asked the campsite staff really nicely, they'd no doubt lend you a saddle so you could take your horse for a gallop along the beach. Imagine it. The sea breeze ruffling your hair, the hooves kicking up wet sand and surf. Well, it would be nice, but it's actually all you can do to get these horses walking away from the campsite. To the known equestrian gaits of walk, trot, canter and gallop, these animals have added the trudge.

But that's probably because they are perfectly happy just to amble along with a caravan behind them. Well, most of them are. One family seemed to have the Irish cousin of a Derby winner pulling them along. I would start out on the road ahead of them each day, only to hear them coming up behind a couple of hours later. I would swerve to the side of the road as they swept past, three faces in a rictus of terror, hands clinging on to the reins in a vain bid to slow down.

If your horse accepts the fiction that you are in charge, however, you are soon lulled into the delights of travelling at horse pace. Sitting on the caravan in the sun, with the rumble of the wheels beneath and the lullaby of the horses hooves on tarmac, it's all too easy to let the eyelids droop. The answer to this, of course, is to walk. And that is really the only way to get the most out of it.

Probably the most important lesson was to keep to the route you are given. Take it from me, horse caravans and hills do not a good mix make. On the final leg, I took a wrong turning and we found ourselves slipping and sliding down a 1 in 8. I had no alternative but to find a turning place and then put my own back into helping the horse back up the hill again. But that, as they say, is all part of the fun.

UNIT 10

Language work

1 What was the writer's main reason for choosing a horse-drawn caravan to travel around Ireland?

2 In your own words, explain what the writer means when he says he became part of the 'tourist landscape'? (lines 14–15)

3 In your own words, explain why the inside of the caravan may have appeared off-putting to some people.

4 Which word in paragraph 2 tells us the writer's attitude towards the size of the caravan?

5 Who or what are the 'uninitiated'? (line 32)

6 In your own words, explain what the writer means by the phrase 'And so to the road'. (line 39)

7 Which phrase in paragraph 4 suggests that the writer's horse was not always completely 'compliant'?

8 Who or what is 'some know-it-all'? (line 45)

9 Which two words does the writer use to describe the typical pace of the horses which pull the caravans?

10 Which expression from paragraph 6 tells us that efforts to control one of the horses were unsuccessful?

11 In your own words, explain why the writer uses the phrase 'accepts the fiction' (line 78) in paragraph 7.

12 In your own words, explain why the writer preferred to walk rather than ride on the caravan.

Summary

In a paragraph of between **75–100 words**, summarize in your own words the problems that the writer suggests people may encounter when travelling around Ireland by horse caravan.

Vocabulary: dealing with topic-specific lexis

1 Look back at the passage. The writer tells us that 'you do not really need any equestrian experience' (lines 40–41). What does he mean by this?

UNIT 10

2 Look at the passage again. Underline the words and phrases which seem to be specific to this area of experience. Divide the words you have found into the following categories. Some words may appear in both columns.

Nouns			Verbs	
_____	_____	_____	_____	_____
_____	_____	_____	_____	_____
_____	_____	_____	_____	
_____	_____			

3 Is it necessary to understand these words in order to:
– answer the questions **1–13** above?
– understand the passage?

4 Why does the writer use these words in the passage?
Who is the intended audience for this passage?

Vocabulary: group nouns

1 In line 24, the writer uses the group noun 'bedding'. Look at the words in the box. How many of the words can we put in the group of things known as 'bedding'?

> blanket   bedside cabinet   curtain   cushion   dressing gown   duvet   headboard   pillow
> mattress   pyjamas   quilt   reading lamp   sleeping bag   valence   pillowcase   bedsocks

2 What groups do the remaining words belong in?

Think of some items that belong in the following groups:

crockery _____

cutlery _____

toiletries _____

stationery _____

soft furnishings _____

3 Can some objects belong to more than one group? Find some examples of such words in the box above.

4 Look back at the passage. The writer uses two other group nouns. Can you find them?

5 Match the group noun on the right with its partner on the left. One has been done for you as an example.

1	a cast	**A**	of trees
2	a range	**B**	of bananas
3	a suite	**C**	of characters
4	a set	**D**	of furniture
5	a bunch	**E**	of whales
6	a team	**F**	of sheep
7	a group	**G**	of hens
8	a school	**H**	of surgeons
9	a clutch	**I**	of mountains
10	a stand	**J**	of companies
11	a flock	**K**	of knives

UNIT 10

USE OF ENGLISH: Transformation sentences 1

Finish each of the following sentences so that it is **as similar as possible in meaning to the sentence printed before it**.

1. I'm more interested in the pay than in the job itself.
   I'm not so _____

2. If you were going to get that job, you'd have heard by now.
   You can't _____

3. The organizers were disappointed by the small number of people attending the conference.
   Much to the _____

4. I wouldn't be at all surprised if that company went bankrupt.
   It would come _____

5. The fuchsias were the only plants to survive the hard winter.
   Apart _____

6. Reports say that the invading army left the city early this morning.
   The invading army _____

7. She looks as if she's been sitting in the sun all day.
   She gives _____

8. As Rod grew older he became less dependent on his family.
   The older _____

9. 'Don't disobey me or I'll stop your pocket money,' said Jane's father.
   Jane's father threatened _____

10. How often do your indoor plants need watering?
    How often is _____

11. The boy went down with chicken pox almost as soon as he'd recovered from measles.
    No sooner _____

12. It was only because she got a bad cough that she gave up smoking.
    But for _____

Transformation sentences 2

For each of the sentences, write a new sentence **as similar as possible in meaning to the original sentence**, but using the word given. This word **must not be altered** in any way.

1. Dave began the race badly because he failed to hear the starter's whistle.
   got
   _____

2. Provided you remain quiet, you can watch the procession from here.
   long
   _____

3. In terms of physical appearance, Henry bears a great resemblance to his father.
   after
   _____

93

UNIT 10

4 The car was parked four hundred metres away from the hotel.
distance

___

5 I inherited this old table from my grandmother.
handed

___

6 Having completed the application form, Jill handed it in to the secretary.
once

___

7 Today's newspaper revealed some interesting facts about a film star.
revelations

___

8 In conclusion, I'd like to make three points.
sum

___

9 Unless you have a licence, you can't drive a car.
possession

___

10 That old market town is worthy of a visit, if you have time.
visiting

___

USE OF ENGLISH: Gap-fill sentences

Fill each of the spaces with a suitable word or phrase.

1 The student got _____ the wrong foot by disagreeing with the teacher.
2 I tried to explain the problem to Bill, but he seems to have got _____ end of the stick entirely.
3 Jeremy's so tactless, every time he opens his mouth he _____ foot in it!
4 Don't buy those apples, Mandy. They look _____ prime.
5 Ben should have _____ than to try and sell stale bread to the baker's wife.
6 Jane is extremely trustworthy, she's not the sort of person to _____ down in any way.
7 Mrs Deacon saw _____ to apologize for her strange behaviour in last week's meeting.
8 I _____ debt of gratitude to Mr Simms who was one of the few people who believed in me when I was wrongfully accused of shoplifting last year.

UNIT 10

PUNCTUATION

Look at this extract from an informal letter written from a woman to a magazine in response to an article about counselling courses. Most of the punctuation has been taken out of the letter.

1. Decide where the sentences start and finish by marking full stops and capital letters on the text.
2. Decide if there are any places where you must put a comma and mark these on the text.
3. Decide if there are any places where you need other marks of punctuation (speech marks, apostrophes, etc.) and mark these on the text.
4. The article was originally divided into 3 paragraphs. Where do you think these came? Why?

> ten or eleven years ago a friend of mine did a counselling course and she used to come round and tell me about the things they did each week i was fairly uninterested and used to think what on earth would anyone want to do a course like that for however when my daughter was in her final year of school and the pressure was on because it was coming up to exam time and she was having difficulties i thought well maybe we need some help here so i rang up the woman who ran the counselling course and my daughter went to see her what she did in a very short time was to completely turn things around my daughter went from being someone who wanted to drop out and give up to someone who was able to face up to things and take responsibility for her own life and i thought thats amazing i want to know what that woman did so i signed up for the counselling course myself

Writing

Now write an introduction and conclusion to the letter. Think about:
- whether the woman is in favour of counselling or not
- what kind of article she might be writing in response to
- what point she is really wanting to make.

SPELLING: Proof reading

Read this text from a tourist brochure. There is a spelling mistake in each line. Underline the word which has been spelled wrongly in each line and write a correction in the space at the end of the line. One has been done for you as an example.

City canals have a particular kind of beauty that makes them <u>magicall.</u>	(0) _magical_
Many writers and poets have been enspired by them with their vague	(1) _____
shapes and muted sounds which give them a mysteriuos quality.	(2) _____
The building of this canal at the beginning of the ninteenth century,	(3) _____
created a seenic enclave much loved by poets and artists. The canal	(4) _____
district has, more recently, become one of the cities most sought-after	(5) _____
residentail areas. And we owe a debt of thanks to the local residents.	(6) _____
Thoughout the years, these people have fought against planners and	(7) _____
developers to keep the atmosfere of the place intact. In the 1950s,	(8) _____
there were tremendous wrows about the replacement of the old gas street	(9) _____
lamps by ugly concreet ones, and also about the cutting down of trees.	(10) _____
In the 1960s, residents fought hard to stop a marina being builded on the	(11) _____
canal, complete with car park and restaraunt in classic 1960s bunker	(12) _____
arcitecture. Looking at the plans now, we can see it as one of the	(13) _____
greatest comunity victories ever won in the city.	(14) _____

UNIT 10

USE OF ENGLISH: Cloze passage

Fill each of the numbered spaces with **one** suitable word. One has been done for you as an example.

Come Rain or Come Shine

It is hard to believe that the British could (**0**) ___have___ greeted the arrival of the umbrella with anything (**1**) _____ enthusiasm. It is, after (**2**) _____, the item which completes the uniform of the City Gent; and the (**3**) _____ of spectators huddling under them at Wimbledon is an enduring image of the British summer. But, (**4**) _____ the umbrella has been used around the world for (**5**) _____ excess of 3000 years, it has only been in the (**6**) _____ 200 years that it has been accepted in Britain.

When, in the 1750s, Jonas Hanway, the philanthropist, traveller and champion (**7**) _____ the umbrella, became the first man (**8**) _____ walk London's streets with one, he was laughed (**9**) _____ and taunted by everyone he met. It took another 50 years (**10**) _____ their appearance at the (**11**) _____ sign of rain became the norm.

It used to be thought that umbrellas were originally (**12**) _____ Chinese invention. But T. S. Crawford, (**13**) _____ of the few umbrella historians, offers Egypt (**14**) _____ its birthplace. He suggests that umbrellas were created (**15**) _____ religious purposes, and that this (**16**) _____ for the object becoming a mark of status in many cultures.

It seems it was the ever-practical Ancient Romans (**17**) _____ first latched onto the umbrella's potential as a shield from the sun or shelter from the rain. Although the British were slow to (**18**) _____ suit, their change of heart when it came was nothing (**19**) _____ not energetic. In 1852, the English inventor, Samuel Fox, created the slim-line frame, still in (**20**) _____ today, which made British umbrellas the most popular in the world.

Answer Key

UNIT 1
Sign of the Times

VOCABULARY: Wordsearch:

1

Horizontal words from the top:
takeaway, cow, omnipresent, *hamburger*, cup, frozen, straw, icon, ground, age, McDonalds, beef, seasoning, fries, chain, coke, bland

Vertical words from left:
Hard Rock Cafe, fastfood, grill, bun, relish, globalize, Hamburg, meat, sesame

2

INGREDIENTS: seasoning, meat, beef, cow
ACCESSORIES: sesame, bun, coke, relish, straw, cup
OPINIONS/IDEAS: omnipresent, icon, globalize, fastfood
PLACES/COMPANIES: Hard Rock Cafe, Hamburg, McDonalds
METHODS/PROCESSES: takeaway, grill, frozen, ground, chain

READING: Planet Pasta

Language work

1. the increasing sales of pasta
2. its simplicity
3. staples
4. it can easily be combined with other things
5. ubiquity
6. it would be difficult to find
7. less formal eating habits
8. modern working hours/women working
9. it was cheap and informal
10. they thought it was a heavy dish/hard to digest
11. the most important reason/explanation
12. The summary should include these ideas:
 – it is easy to cook and prepare
 – it can be combined with other flavours
 – it is cheap, filling and nutritious
 – everyone seems to like it
 – eating habits/customs have changed
 – people concerned about having a healthy diet

Reference skills

1. pasta
2. flavours
3. Italy
4. factors
5. mealtimes/symbolic importance of mealtimes
6. this new ease of eating
7. quick fixes
8. the fact that pasta has made great strides

Dependent prepositions

1. from
2. of
3. with
4. with
5. from
6. to
7. into
8. to

GRAMMAR: Causatives

1. have this document translated into English.
2. have trousers shortened at the cleaners.
3. have your central heating boiler serviced annually.
4. have my passport photo taken by a professional photographer.
5. have the food for the party prepared by a catering company.
6. to have it repaired by an engineer, you can do it yourself.
7. are having a new set of dining-room curtains made.
8. have had the outside of the house painted by a gardener.
9. been having my hair cut by Louise for years.
10. to have those trees cut down, ask Tom Smith.
11. to have a filling/a tooth filled at the dentist's.
12. could have had your new sofa delivered on Monday.

HELP WITH PUNCTUATION 1:
Full stops & capital letters

Suggested answer

*As any **I**talian housewife will tell you, homemade pasta is not difficult to make. **I**t does, however, require patience and time, which is why **I** tend to make it on Sunday mornings. **P**eople who have a gift for making pastry or bread will have very little problem in making pasta as many of the skills applied to all three are the same. **T**he most important thing to remember is that you need plenty of uncluttered work surface. **A** very large chopping board or marble slab is ideal, but modern laminate worktops are quite adequate. **A**n extra large rolling pin will make the rolling of the pasta dough much easier. **I**f you plan to go into pasta making in a big way, then it may be worth your while to buy a pasta machine. **A**t the turn of a handle, this will give you many different shapes and thicknesses of pasta. **T**hese machines, manufactured in northern **I**taly, are now widely available in specialist kitchenware shops all over the world.*

PHRASAL VERBS with *out*

1. come
2. bringing
3. draw
4. fallen
5. got
6. hold
7. sold
8. watch
9. called
10. pulling

ANSWER KEY

WRITING: Linking words and phrases
1 B
2 B
3 C
4 A
5 D
6 D
7 B
8 C
9 A
10 C
11 C
12 D

HELP WITH SPELLING 1: the silent e
1 immediately
2 smiling
3 amazement
4 changeable
5 seeing
6 shining
7 barely
8 agreement
9 management/manager/manageress
10 lovely
11 definitely

GRAMMAR: Review of past tenses
1 was
2 had been
3 had always had
4 had never
5 had been getting
6 decided
7 was
8 turned
9 had
10 was
11 has suffered
12 has never had
13 signed
14 had started
15 (had) realized
16 needed
17 had
18 was
19 has been
20 have begun

USE OF ENGLISH: Cloze passage
1 way
2 to
3 try
4 out
5 with
6 in
7 who
8 up
9 what
10 during
11 sending
12 take
13 been
14 against
15 came
16 contents
17 created
18 of
19 the
20 times

Vocabulary
1 unfounded
2 outraged
3 shattered
4 shards
5 sabotage
6 grudge
7 stank
8 culprit

UNIT 2 Call of the Wild

VOCABULARY: Wordsearch

1

Horizontal words from the top:
python, frog, bird, snake, parrot, cat, mouse, fox, rabbit, bat, gnu, duck, owl, dodo, ox, orang utan, fly, tokapi, sheep, dachshund, lamb, bull, wasp, deer

Vertical words from the left:
puppy, whale, tarantula, fish, boa, horse, scorpion, mule, dog, chipmunk, bee, pig, chicken, rat, labrador

2
MAMMALS: cat, mouse, fox, rabbit, bat, gnu, ox, orang utan, tokapi, sheep, dachshund, lamb, bull, deer, puppy, whale, horse, dog, chipmunk, pig, rat, labrador, mule
BIRDS: chicken, parrot, owl, duck, dodo
REPTILES/AMPHIBIANS: boa, frog, snake, python
INSECTS: bee, wasp, fly,
OTHERS: fish, scorpion, tarantula

4 as blind as a bat
as busy as a bee
as free as a bird
as sick as a parrot
as proud as a peacock
as quiet as a mouse
as sly as a fox
as strong as an ox
as stubborn as a mule
as wise as an owl

READING: Day of the sparrow

Comprehension
1 D
2 D
3 C
4 B
5 A

Vocabulary
1 ousting
2 in time
3 inkling
4 unscathed
5 boom
6 stowaways
7 annoyances
8 hallmark
9 foliage
10 drive out
11 keep in check
12 nipped in the bud
13 juggernaut

Reference skills
1 visiting a new island
2 what is happening around them
3 the rate of species introductions
4 introduced species
5 grass introduced from Africa
6 blocking the movement of species likely to cause problems
7 problem species

Word families and wordstress

8
1 de<u>press</u>   de<u>press</u>ion   de<u>press</u>ing
2 <u>glob</u>alize   <u>globe</u>   <u>glob</u>al
3 in<u>vade</u>   in<u>vas</u>ion   in<u>vad</u>ing/in<u>vas</u>ive
4 pre<u>vent</u>   pre<u>vent</u>ion   pre<u>vent</u>ative
5 *invading* describes an action; *invasive* describes a quality.
6 *surprised* describes a person's reaction to something; *surprising* describes a quality of something.

9
1 e<u>col</u>ogy   eco<u>log</u>ical
2 ca<u>tas</u>trophe   cata<u>stroph</u>ic
3 <u>con</u>tinent   conti<u>nen</u>tal
4 <u>pho</u>tograph   photo<u>graph</u>ic
5 bi<u>ol</u>ogy   bio<u>log</u>ical

10
1 ho<u>mog</u>enize   homogeni<u>za</u>tion
2 <u>pop</u>ulate   popu<u>la</u>tion
3 <u>dev</u>astate   deva<u>sta</u>tion
4 <u>is</u>olate   iso<u>la</u>tion
5 <u>nat</u>uralize   naturali<u>za</u>tion
6 <u>in</u>filtrate   infil<u>tra</u>tion
7 <u>punc</u>tuate   punctu<u>a</u>tion
8 pro<u>nounce</u>   pronunci<u>a</u>tion

ANSWER KEY

GRAMMAR: Relative pronouns

1 Suggested answers
1 Sparrows are birds which…
2 Wendy Stahm is a scientist who…
3 Lantana is a plant which…
4 Howard Mooney is a scientist who…
5 New Zealand is a country where…
6 African grasses are introduced species which…

2 Suggested answers
1 The parrot (which) I saw in the shop was exactly the type I wanted.
2 The prawns (which) we had for lunch must have been off.
3 There was a popular soap-opera in the Far East which starred an orang-utan.
4 Many whales turn up on beaches where there are no people.
5 I knocked on the door which looked like the right one.
6 I wanted to make a film which would highlight the problems of dolphins.
7 John Small is the name of the man who sold me the tarantula.
8 The spider which has escaped from the zoo is thought to be very dangerous.
9 *Bleak House* is probably the best novel which Dickens ever wrote.
10 People who are interested in animal welfare are invited to join the organization.
11 A new pet shop where you can buy snakes has just opened.
12 I never thought I'd see such a thing as an orang-utan which could play the piano.

GRAMMAR: Use of the article

1 a
2 a
3 the
4 a/the
5 –
6 a
7 the
8 the
9 the
10 –
11 –
12 –
13 the
14 the

HELP WITH SPELLING 2: Double consonants

1 marketing
2 knitted
3 spinning
4 developing
5 beginning
6 committed
7 dropped
8 occurred
9 transferring
10 permitted/permissible
11 conference

GRAMMAR: Expressing cause and result

Suggested answers
1 Illness or injury is often the cause of whale strandings.
2 The introduction of African grasses resulted in more frequent fires.
3 Isolation often leads to the creation of new species.
4 Pollution may be to blame for the dolphin's loss of immunity to the virus.
5 Mass strandings are often the result of disorientation.
6 Pollution cannot always be blamed for environmental disasters.
7 A TV programme has led to the latest fashion for exotic pets.
8 Hunting is thought to have been the cause of the extinction of the dodo.

PHRASAL VERBS: with *up* and *down*

1 backed
2 feel
3 catch
4 bring
5 do
6 drawn
7 held
8 made
9 ran
10 set

HELP WITH PUNCTUATION 2: Commas

Suggested answer

27, Acacia Avenue
Harmborough
Surrey

The Manager
Pet City
Manchester

Dear Sir,

Recently, I read an article which said that Pet City was the best place to buy tarantulas. As I would like to buy one as a pet, I am writing to ask if you have any in stock at the moment.

Unfortunately, I have never had a pet spider before, so I was wondering if you could send me some information about the best way to look after them. For example, are your tarantulas sold with cages and bedding or do I have to pay for these separately? I already have a pet dog and a small python but no other spiders. Do you think my tarantula will be lonely? Should I buy two or will that lead to other problems?

I would be grateful to receive the answer to these questions together with your pricelist, a brochure, any other information you may have about tarantulas and details of how to get to your shop from the city centre.

Yours faithfully,

A. Strangelove

VOCABULARY: Idiomatic use of animal vocabulary

1 dogged
2 badgered
3 foxed
4 fishing
5 worm

FORMAL AND INFORMAL LANGUAGE

1 writing
2 further
3 organize
4 noticed
5 advertisement
6 surprised
7 the wide range
8 on offer
9 feel sure
10 be exactly what I am looking for
11 grateful
12 to receive
13 latest
14 together with
15 hearing from you
16 sincerely

UNIT 3
A Word in your Ear

IDIOMATIC EXPRESSIONS

1 B
2 C
3 A
4 D
5 C
6 B
7 D
8 A
9 B
10 B

ANSWER KEY

READING: Mind your language

Language work
1 The UK is the centre of international business, but the local workforce is not good at languages.
2 plummeting (= decreasing rapidly)
3 first point of contact
4 People may not feel comfortable using the telephone.
5 Because the telephone requires an immediate response.
6 (a) grounding
7 Pretending to be in certain situations.
8 To make social conversation with someone.
9 Where two people speaking to each other fail to understand each other.
10 exhilarating
11 The way people move, or their posture and gestures, which can be interpreted to mean different things in different cultures.
12 That social conventions do not travel across cultures.

Summary
The summary should include the following main points:
Secretaries should
– learn to cope on the telephone
– learn limited phrases for specific purposes
– learn to identify the language being spoken
– learn to offer basic hospitality
– learn about other cultures

Reference skills
1 coping on the telephone in another language
2 using the telephone
3 Rendezvous
4 learning limited phrases/acting out scenarios
5 identify the language/give a simple message
6 those that give a simple message, e.g. *hang on*
7 a joke or light-hearted remark

Wordstress
1
1 se<u>c</u>retary
2 inter<u>na</u>tional
3 communi<u>ca</u>tion
4 organi<u>za</u>tion
5 <u>coll</u>eague
6 repu<u>ta</u>tion
7 super<u>fi</u>cially
8 lin<u>gui</u>stic
9 con<u>sul</u>tant
10 con<u>duc</u>ting
11 in<u>ti</u>midating
12 <u>in</u>strument
13 im<u>me</u>diacy
14 tu<u>i</u>tion
15 nece<u>ssa</u>rily
16 ex<u>hi</u>larating
17 <u>com</u>plicated
18 hospi<u>ta</u>lity
19 sensi<u>bi</u>lity
20 po<u>ten</u>tial

2

■ ■ ■
secretary
instrument

■ ■ ■ ■
complicated

■ ■ ■
conducting
potential
linguistic
consultant
tuition

■ ■ ■ ■
reputation

■ ■ ■ ■ ■
intimidating
exhilarating
immediacy

■ ■ ■ ■ ■
superficially
sensibility
international
hospitality
necessarily

■ ■ ■ ■ ■
organization
communication

HELP WITH PUNCTUATION 3: Apostrophes and genitives

1 Please don't waste everybody else's time as well as ours.
2 I haven't bought anything for the twins' birthday yet.
3 It isn't the sort of thing that suits Bill and Fiona's taste.
4 The city's full of shops selling tomorrow's fashions today.
5 Some children's clothes are sold upstairs, others are to be found in teenage fashions.
6 Linda's appointment is at four o'clock and Robert's follows hers, but you're not on today's list, I'm afraid.
7 We'll have to make sure that Mr Peters' watch says the same time as ours.
8 It's high time the sports club did something about its members' changing facilities.
9 Tom's mother's house isn't as old as its appearance suggests, her neighbours' houses are older.
10 Theirs is the village's most beautiful garden and there's no doubt it's larger than anybody else's too.

GRAMMAR: The passive voice
Suggested answers
1 is said to be friendly with a number of well-known celebrities.
2 is generally thought to have done a good job.
3 is widely considered to be the best dentist in town.
4 new law banning traffic from the city centre is going to be introduced.
5 President is alleged to be considering marriage.
6 dough has to be left for a couple of hours before baking.
7 ought to have been informed that the train would be delayed.
8 students were distracted from the lecture by a large wasp.
9 wrong man is widely believed to have been accused of the murder.
10 should the electricity meter be touched.
11 singer is rumoured to be planning to sell his house.
12 date had been fixed for the meeting, few people bothered to come.

MAKING SUGGESTIONS
Suggested answers
1 Melanie suggested (that) Tom (should) join an animal welfare group.
2 I suggest that Terry should buy his own car.
3 Lyn has suggested (that) we (should) get a cat.
Lyn has suggested getting a cat.
4 Anna suggested (that) they went/should go to the cinema on Saturday night.
Anna suggested going to the cinema on Saturday night.
5 Pat suggested that Wendy was working too hard.
6 Darren suggested that we (should) go/(that) we went whale watching.
Darren suggested going whale watching.
7 Tracy said that Sharon should start looking for a job.
Tracy suggested that Sharon started looking for a job.
8 Emma suggested (that) they (should) get Grandma a tarantula for her birthday.
Emma suggested (that) they got Grandma a tarantula for her birthday.
Emma suggested getting Grandma a tarantula for her birthday.

ANSWER KEY

9 It was suggested (that) I (should) take up fishing.
It was suggested (that) I took up fishing.
10 Billy suggested stopping for a cup of tea.
Billy suggested (that) they (should) stop for a cup of tea.

HELP WITH SPELLING 3:
Words ending in *y*

1
1 reliance
2 denial
3 application
4 nastiness
5 implication
6 laziness
7 defiance
8 bullying
9 dryness
10 loveliness

2
1 toys
2 trolleys
3 quarries
4 puppies
5 highways
6 holidays
7 pennies
8 displays
9 spies
10 fairies

VOCABULARY: Similes

1 pretty
2 fresh
3 stubborn
4 right
5 light
6 bright
7 quick
8 fit
9 peas
10 black

USE OF ENGLISH:
My chequered career

Cloze passage
1 about
2 who
3 should
4 attracting
5 into
6 way
7 do
8 Indeed
9 affair
10 not
11 running
12 between
13 as

14 since
15 were
16 pick
17 stick
18 one
19 in
20 likely

Comprehension
1 Yes
2 Yes
3 No
4 Yes
5 No
6 No
7 Yes
8 Yes
9 No
10 No

GRAMMAR:
Comparison and contrast

Suggested answers
1 Unlike some other European languages, English makes great use of the passive.
2 Although computers save a lot of time, learning to use one can be very time-consuming.
3 Whilst the demand for cookery books is rising, that for quiz books remains stable.
4 In comparison with other areas, our local bus service is very regular.
5 Despite raining heavily/the fact that it rained heavily for a short time, the garden party was a great success.
6 Far from being expensive, the price of eating out in Glasgow is actually quite reasonable.
7 In spite of having/the fact that he had a slight head cold, James sang beautifully at Jessica's wedding.
8 Whereas the coach takes five hours to get to London, the train does it in two and a half hours.
9 However much you may dislike folk music, I'm sure you'll like this particular band.
10 Although hill walking is tiring, it doesn't require as much concentration as mountain climbing.
11 I know you're not keen on Italian food, nonetheless I think you should try a piece of polenta.
12 Although my car is not easy to drive, it does not demand the same degree of skill in the driver as yours.

WRITING: Translations

1 omit *they*
2 of (*to* = wrong prepostion)
3 omit *to*
4 to (*at* = wrong prepostion)

5 furnished (spelling)
6 to (*up* = wrong preposition)
7 omit *to*
8 at (*for* = wrong preposition)
9 length (spelling)
10 price (spelling)
11 under/up to (*till* = wrong preposition)
12 admitted (spelling)

UNIT 4
A Fine Romance

VOCABULARY: Wordsearch

1
Horizontal words from the top:
modesty, brave, cautious, wise, loyal, *loving*, intelligence, trust, hero, style, moody, nosy, nasty, sexy, generosity, bossy, talented, sulky, charm, judgement

Vertical from the left:
commonsense, witty, honesty, bright, nice, patience, bully, reliability, fit

2

POSITIVE ADJECTIVES	POSITIVE NOUNS
brave	→ bravery
cautious	→ caution
wise	→ wisdom
loyal	→ loyalty
sexy	→ sex
talented	→ talent
witty	→ wit
bright	→ brightness
nice	→ niceness
fit	→ fitness

NEGATIVE ADJECTIVES	NEGATIVE NOUNS
moody	→ mood/moodiness
nosy	→ nosiness
nasty	→ nastiness
bossy	→ bossiness
sulky	→ sulker/sulkiness

POSITIVE NOUNS	POSITIVE ADJECTIVES
modesty	→ modest
intelligence	→ intelligent
trust	→ trusting/trustworthy
hero	→ heroic
style	→ stylish
generosity	→ generous
charm	→ charming
commonsense	→ sensible
honesty	→ honest
patience	→ patient
reliability	→ reliable

ANSWER KEY

NEGATIVE NOUNS	NEGATIVE ADJECTIVES
judgement →	judgemental
bully →	bullied

READING: The agony and the ecstasy

Comprehension
1. C
2. C
3. B
4. A
5. D

Vocabulary
1. dispensing
2. to offer guidance
3. foolhardy
4. strife
5. makes no bones
6. outspoken
7. dished out
8. dogma
9. irrepressible
10. strike a chord
11. relishes
12. vital, essential

Wordstress
1. <u>coun</u>sellor
2. psy<u>chol</u>ogist
3. re<u>la</u>tionship
4. per<u>cep</u>tion
5. pro<u>fes</u>sionalism
6. curi<u>os</u>ity
7. out<u>spo</u>ken
8. irre<u>press</u>ible
8. com<u>pul</u>sion
10. qualifi<u>ca</u>tions
11. unbe<u>liev</u>ably
12. es<u>sen</u>tial

Summary
The summary should include these ideas:
– Irma has no particular philosophy or set of beliefs
– have the confidence to solve your own problems
– don't always expect others to help you
– don't assume that your experience is unique
– don't assume others have had the same experiences as you
– don't forget to look after the things that are most important to you

NARRATIVE DEVICES: Inversion

Suggested answers
1. Seldom does one get the chance to meet famous writers.
2. No longer will the bus stop outside the post office.
3. Hardly ever do I stop to count the number of cups of coffee I drink.
4. Hardly had John had time to take his seat in the cinema than the lights went out.
5. Scarcely ever do you see owls during the daytime.
6. Never in my whole life have I experienced such an uncomfortable journey.
7. Not often do you get offered an opportunity like that.
8. Under no circumstances should this letter be opened.
9. Not a soul did Richard meet as he walked into town.
10. Only when I saw the look on her face did I realize what I'd said.

HELP WITH SPELLING 4: Common errors

1. principles
2. break
3. advice
4. dessert
5. lose, loose
6. practice
7. stationary
8. whether
9. quite
10. passed
11. formerly
12. beside

USE OF ENGLISH: Cloze passage

Suggested answers
1. with
2. to
3. likely
4. in
5. hold
6. depend
7. into
8. do
9. of
10. its
11. and
12. called/termed
13. (Al)Though/While/Whilst
14. how
15. the
16. out
17. as/though
18. an
19. sources
20. than

VOCABULARY: Uses of *get*

Suggested answers
1. Tom and Carly got married on Saturday.
2. Jane got the blame/got blamed for the mistake.
3. Rosy gets upset very easily.
4. I would like to get on better with my neighbours.
5. Susan yawned because she was getting bored with the play/because the play was getting boring.
6. Terry got told off by his teacher yesterday.
7. During the fight a large window got broken.
8. After ten minutes waiting, Kathy began to get depressed.
After ten minutes, waiting began to get Kathy down.
9. Increasingly, Sally's behaviour was getting on Peter's nerves.
10. Simon should get that broken tooth looked at by a dentist.

GRAMMAR: Structure words

1. without
2. those
3. All
4. This
5. at least
6. especially
7. However
8. only
9. when
10. Yet
11. Despite
12. And

Language work
1. 3, 2
2. all, a series like this
3. *and, with; however* clause
4. The style is found in more formal/journalistic writing.
5. It is economical through its use of noun phrases which express complex ideas in a simple way. It gives variety of style and structure.
6. *less-informed readers, the rigid format, no other art history series as wide-ranging, well-researched and up-to-date, invariably experts in their field*

HELP WITH PUNCTUATION 4: Inverted commas

Robert looked down at the hole in his pullover. **'**What am I going to tell auntie**?'** ,he said. **'**Tell her you lost it,**'** I suggested **'**she'll knit you another.**'**
Robert didn't look convinced and was trying to take off the remains of his pullover. **'H**ang on a moment,**'** I said **'I'll** help you.**'**
I hadn't heard footsteps or the gate opening but suddenly I heard **M**iss Locke's voice enquiring icily, **'**What on earth is going on here**?'**

ANSWER KEY

USE OF ENGLISH: Cloze passage

1. yourself
2. with
3. for
4. by
5. own
6. in
7. taken
8. laid
9. chances/rate
10. surrounds/encircles/encloses
11. there
12. would
13. into
14. out
15. just/only
16. on
17. as
18. if
19. whom
20. down

IDIOMATIC EXPRESSIONS

Suggested answers
1. When she talks about herself like that it really gets on my nerves.
2. All this talk of marital disharmony (really) gets me down.
3. We'll have to get a move on if we're going to catch that bus.
4. Renata gets a lot of enjoyment out of looking after children.
5. I can't (seem to) get my head round this instruction booklet.
6. David doesn't seem to be able to get to grips with the new computer system.
7. Angela is just getting over a nasty bout of flu.
8. Maggie's little boy is just learning to get dressed by himself.
9. That little joke really got me into deep water.
10. Molly finds it difficult to get used to the idea that her daughter is grown up.

UNIT 5
All Right on the Night

READING:
Who's a pretty plant then?

Pre-reading task

name after = to give something or someone a name which is known to be already associated with something or someone else.

Use of the article

1. the
2. the
3. a
4. a
5. the
6. a
7. the
8. a
9. a
10. an
11. the
12. the
13. an
14. the
15. a
16. the
17. A
18. B
19. A
20. C
21. A
22. A
23. B
24. A
25. C
26. A
27. A
28. C

Reference skills

1. the latinization of names
2. the latinization of names
3. by having a plant named after them
4. a popular celebrity
5. Barry Dare
6. name it after yourself
7. commercial companies
8. with your name
9. the plant

Vocabulary

1. acclaim
2. latterly
3. on occasion
4. in years gone by
5. chic
6. fitting
7. feted
8. hard and fast
9. come up with the cash

Summary

The summary should include these ideas:
– named after a famous person to honour them
– named after a famous person to get publicity for the plant
– named after a relative of the plant breeder
– named after a product as a form of advertising
– you can buy a variety and name it after yourself

GRAMMAR: Clauses with *whatever, however,* etc.

1. much it costs/may cost, I'm determined to complete the project.
2. unpopular it may make him, John always sticks to his principles.
3. else you do while you're in London, go to the National Gallery.
4. film she appears in, she always seems to play the same character.
5. road you take, they all end up at the same place.
6. you go in the city, you see wonderful examples of modern architecture.
7. I see Sally in that dress I'm reminded of Marilyn Monroe.
8. many people you ask, I'm sure you'll get the same answer.

SPELLING & PRONUNCIATION

1
1. thorough
2. thought
3. through
4. tough
5. troughs
6. Throughout
7. distraught
8. though

2

PORT	CRAFT	STUFF
taught	draught	enough
sought	coughed	trough
distraught	laughed	rough
nought		tough
fraught		
caught		
ought		

3
1. sort
2. court
3. course
4. foul
5. idol
6. peace
7. source
8. bridal
9. aisle
10. bear
11. fares
12. waste

GRAMMAR: Reported speech

1 Suggested answers
1. asked Liz if she knew Mr Trout's phone number.
2. reporter asked the woman what time the fight (had) started.
3. asked Mandy how her sister was getting on at her new school.

103

ANSWER KEY

4 father asked her to pass him the newspaper.
5 explained to Rosie that he was having his car serviced the following/next day and so (he) couldn't give her a lift.
6 sports commentator said he/she thought it was going to be a day to remember.
7 told Tom that he'd have to ring him back later as/because there was somebody knocking at the door.
8 receptionist asked the man to repeat his surname.
9 asked Terry to get Josie to ring her after lunch.

2 Suggested answers
1 'Now could you tell me exactly what happened, please?' said the reporter to the woman who'd been mugged.
2 'How many times have you answered/did you answer the phone this/that evening?' the police officer asked Mrs Hilary.
3 'Would you like to go to the party with me, Sharon?' asked Phil.
4 'Are you enjoying your new job, Denise?' I asked.
5 'I can't sing tonight because I've just had a tooth out,' I explained to the band.
6 'How long will it take to get to the cinema, Mike?' asked Annette.
7 'I'm very disappointed that no one asked/has asked my opinion,' said Richard.
8 'Why wasn't I invited to last week's meeting, Mr French?' asked Diane.
9 'I would like to thank all those who sent me good wishes during my illness last year,' said Simon.

VOCABULARY: Wordsearch

Horizontal words from the top:
comedy, plot, drama, *romance*, horror, opera, musical, tragedy, character, Oscar, director, style, folk, video, narrative, stage, performance

Vertical words from the left:
cartoon, rock, play, mime, hero, dance, act, pop, media, jazz, love, costume, part, studio, image, catalogue, thriller

WRITING:
Grease is not such a smash hit

Cloze passage
1 A
2 C
3 C
4 A
5 A
6 B
7 D

8 B
9 B
10 C
11 A
12 B
13 A
14 D
15 B

Comprehension
1
1 T
2 T
3 F
4 F
5 T
6 F

2 Suggested answers
1 probably 8-10
2 probably 2-4
3 probably 4-6
4 probably 6-8
5 probably 2-4

3
1 introduction/this restaurant placed in its context
2 the decor
3 a special feature
4 the meal
5 the conclusion

4 Suggested answers
1 mostly opinion
2 mostly description
3 about 50/50
4 about 50/50
5 mostly opinion

5 newspaper/magazine
6 would-be diners

7 fairly informal (e.g. *the trouble…is, it's not bad!*) slightly ironic in tone (e.g. *The only taste…was a bitter one*)

USE OF ENGLISH: Cloze passage

Suggested answers
1 From
2 for
3 with
4 like
5 into
6 who/which/that
7 But
8 what
9 or
10 of
11 spend
12 took
13 up
14 used
15 not
16 in
17 tends/seems
18 doesn't

19 case
20 as

UNIT 6
Tip of my Tongue

READING: The making of memory

Comprehension
1 A
2 B
3 A
4 C
5 B
6 D
7 C

Vocabulary
1 conjure up
2 trajectory
3 amnesia
4 advocates
5 prodigious
6 hindrance
7 chimera
8 humiliation
9 trivia
10 envisage
11 tally
12 embedded

Reference skills
1 our capacity for memory
2 the dead
3 advocates of cryonics
4 our memories
5 memories
6 photograph
7 past experiences
8 forgetting is functional
9 nerve cells
10 in the human brain
11 cells
12 persist

Wordstress
1 characte<u>ris</u>tic
2 il<u>lu</u>minated
3 un<u>know</u>able
4 ac<u>com</u>panied
5 humili<u>a</u>tion
6 ap<u>point</u>ment
7 co<u>nnec</u>tion
8 em<u>bed</u>ded
9 recogni<u>sa</u>bly
10 consti<u>tu</u>ent
11 <u>sub</u>tleties
12 com<u>po</u>nents

104

ANSWER KEY

Prefixes and suffixes

1 en\code\d   em\bed\ded
2 To construct the passive: *'Are all our past experiences…encoded…'*, *'our memories, (which are) embedded…'*
3 before certain consonants, e.g. p/b. More examples include: *improve, imbalance, embody, embark.*

GRAMMAR: Gerund and infinitive

1
1 to memorize
2 going
3 to remember
4 to try
5 making
6 Memorizing
7 using
8 to learn
9 to call
10 hearing
11 to find
12 to ask

2

A (+infinitive)	B (+ gerund)
plan	avoid
offer	resist
intend	face
want	miss
decide	regret
expect	finish
refuse	risk
hope	mention
learn	forgive
regret	postpone
	consider
	admit

PUNCTUATION: Commas and clauses

1 Before beginning work for the day *(clause)*, Tom *(subject)* turned on his computer.
2 First of all *(clause)*, I'd *(subject)* like to talk about my own experience.
3 Surprising as it may seem *(clause)*, memories *(subject)* are our most enduring characteristics.
4 Apart from Dr Brown *(clause)*, nobody *(subject)* knew how to programme the computer.
5 You *(subject)* can borrow my BMW, as long as you drive carefully *(clause)*.
6 Far from being cold in the room *(clause)*, it *(subject)* turned out to be rather warm.
7 Had it not been for Barbara's help *(clause)*, the project *(subject)* would never have been completed.
8 The party *(subject)* will be held in the open air, providing that it doesn't rain *(clause)*.
9 Unless you *(subject)* have any objections *(clause)*, the meeting will take place on March 4th.
10 Despite the limited time available for rehearsals *(clause)*, the band *(subject)* seemed very well prepared.

READING

Pre-reading task

1
A one action followed by another
B defining relative clause identifies the subject
C change of subject means victim and attacker change roles
2 third one is probably more difficult because of the grammar
4 A
5 Did the reporter attack the senator? to see if they had understood the grammar/how long they took to work out the meaning

Language work

1 They are types of puzzles designed to test your powers of reasoning. People are motivated to solve the problems, but are often frustrated by their level of difficulty.
2 quickly starts to work
3 something anyone can understand readily
4 understanding of complex things
5 that the brain works harder to solve difficult problems
6 which part of the brain deals with such problems
7 because this involves a wide variety of knowledge
8 getting more complex as you go down the list
9 it took longer to read, caused their pupils to dilate more and was more likely to be misunderstood
10 left, there are two areas here which may be responsible for processing meaning and associated sounds

Grammar: relative pronouns

1 Third sentence. It is possible to use *whom* when it refers to the object of the sentence.

2
1 A
2 C
3 C
4 B
5 A
6 B
7 B
8 C
9 C
10 C

3
1 from
2 with
3 to
4 to
5 To
6 Tom is the man (who) I bought my old car from.
7 Polly is a student (who) I communicate with on the Internet.
8 What's the name of the person (who) you sent that fax to?
9 Lizzie is the girl (who) we gave our old desktop computer to.
10 Who do I have the pleasure of speaking to?

4
1 which
2 whom/who
3 which
4 whom
5 whom/who
6 where
7 which
8 where
9 who
10 which

GRAMMAR: Conditional sentences

Suggested answers
1 If I were you/in your place, I'd report the incident to the police.
2 Had you taken my advice, you wouldn't be in this mess now.
3 Unless somebody asks to see your passport, say nothing.
4 Should it (happen to) rain, the party will be held indoors.
5 Unless anyone disagrees, the meeting planned for next week will be cancelled.
6 As long as you get plenty of practice of driving, you are likely to pass the test.
7 Should you ever be in need of assistance, let me know.
8 Whether the children are ready or not, dinner will be served at eight.
9 Providing prices don't rise dramatically, we'll be able to afford a new car next year.
10 Whether there's a lot of wind or not, we'll go sailing tomorrow.

SPELLING: Proof reading

1 makeing → making
2 reveled → revealed
3 webb → web
4 developped → developed
5 won → one
6 know → known

ANSWER KEY

7 diferent → different
8 responsable → responsible
9 acording → according
10 relavent → relevant
11 geting → getting
12 brian → brain
13 scull → skull
14 additionaly → additionally

VOCABULARY: Wordsearch

Horizontal words from the top:
computer, CD Rom(s), site, default, flame, internet, printer, save, lurk, bbfn (abbreviation of *bye-bye for now*), command, keyboard, drive, wordprocessor

Vertical words from the left:
logon, mouse, e-mail, copy, network, menu, terminal, font, key, ram, modem, fax, download, click, laptop, file, exit, word, floppy, disk, database, spreadsheet, edit

UNIT 7
A Matter of Taste

VOCABULARY: Wordsearch

1 Horizontal words from the top:
scarves, jacket, leggings, denim, money, shawl, belt, silk, wool, trainers, leather, earring, boilersuit

Vertical words from the left:
sequins, bowtie, cotton, lycra, vest, tie, cardigan, slippers, jeans, socks, fur, tattoo, (over)coat, brooch, braces, anorak, baseball cap, polyester

2
ARTICLES OF CLOTHING: jacket, leggings, trainers, boilersuit, vest, cardigan, slippers, jeans, socks, (over)coat, anorak
ACCESSORIES: scarves, money, shawl, belt, earring, sequins, bowtie, tie, tattoo, brooch, braces, baseball cap
MATERIALS: denim, silk, wool, leather, cotton, fur, polyester, lycra

USE OF ENGLISH: Cloze passage

Suggested answers
1 all
2 each/every
3 to
4 from/are
5 such
6 one
7 in
8 but/while/yet
9 for

10 which/that
11 when/as
12 by
13 there
14 on
15 idea
16 up
17 highly/very/extremely
18 of
19 into
20 both

Language work

1–4

POSITIVE ADJECTIVE	POSITIVE NOUN
ver*satile*	versa*tility*
in*genious*	in*geniousness*
elegant	*elegance*
*val*uable	*val*ue

NEGATIVE ADJECTIVE	NEGATIVE NOUN
least a*cclaimed*	a*cclaim*
scruffy	*scruffiness*
out*moded*	

NEUTRAL ADJECTIVE	NEUTRAL NOUN
bold	boldness
ephemeral	ephemera

GRAMMAR: Gerund versus infinitive

1 going
2 mentioning
3 to accept
4 to invest
5 to learn
6 travelling
7 to mention
8 to borrow
9 tidying
10 listening
11 to catch
12 to see
13 to agree
14 suggesting
15 visiting
16 criticizing
17 getting
18 to be
19 to take
20 being

HELP WITH SPELLING 5: cede/ceed/sede

1 successful
2 preceding
3 recede
4 superseded
5 judgement
6 speed
7 personal
8 proceedings

USE OF ENGLISH: Structure words

1 where
2 or
3 even
4 for
5 but
6 unless
7 among
8 the
9 with
10 and
11 with
12 such as
13 over
14 where
15 almost

VOCABULARY: Prefixes with *up*

1 upset
2 upkeep
3 uphill
4 upside
5 uptake
6 uptight
7 upturn
8 update
9 upright
10 upshot

GRAMMAR: Wishes & regrets

Suggested answers
1 he could have gone to the football match.
2 she had sent a postcard to her family when she was on holiday.
3 wish Raphaella good luck in her exams the next/following day.
4 Graham wished he didn't have to visit his grandmother.
5 Dennis wishes he was/were better at maths.
6 Pamela wishes she could/was allowed to stay out later on Saturday night.
7 Ronnie wishes Samantha would help him with his homework.
8 Kelly wishes it would stop raining.
9 Benny wishes he could speak Welsh.
10 Patsy wishes she hadn't said that her sister's boyfriend was stupid.
11 I wish you could have come to the party, it was great.
12 I wish (that) Racquel wouldn't keep leaving the door open.

ANSWER KEY

READING: Let's not fight about it

Comprehension
1 C
2 C
3 A
4 D
5 B

Language work
1 outburst
2 The incident has stayed with me...
3 That this culture is based on opposition rather than co-operation.
4 Because it actually fails to do this and only focuses on extremes.
5 invective
6 ubiquity
7 That violence/violent reactions do not help us understand each other/things better.
8 That it has become a habit/that it is now the expected norm.
9 harvest

Vocabulary
1 hurling
2 prize
3 knee-jerk
4 tactics
5 get in the way of
6 rears its head

Reference skills
1 his attack
2 the man who was a co-guest on the TV show
3 the incident
4 ritualized opposition
5 extreme views
6 taking up positions
7 a standard way of writing an academic paper
8 people holding contrary views to one's own
9 this ethic of aggression

Summary
The summary should include these ideas:
– a lot of aggression/opposition in public debate
– many believe that argument is the best way to resolve an issue
– people may come to value aggression for its own sake
– people may behave more aggressively than they feel
– solutions may actually be more difficult to find if people are aggressive
– people may feel guilty about compromise/co-operation
– aggressive attitudes lead to other sorts of anti-social behaviour

USE OF ENGLISH: Inversions
Suggested answers
1 as this car may have been to buy, it wasn't good value.
2 though this hotel is, it lacks the atmosphere of its neighbour.
3 though the painting is, it doesn't compare with the great masters.
4 as it may seem, Polly has no formal artistic training.
5 in the 18th century, the house is very well kept.
6 good at painting, Fred actually specializes in making furniture.
7 engrossed was Gerry in his novel that he forgot the loaf he'd put in the oven.
8 to my expectations, Daphne arrived at the hotel in good time.
9 Gail to be a fan of the group, I wasn't surprised to see her at the concert.
10 from being interested in classical music, Tony rather likes jazz.
11 bad was Sally's timekeeping that she risked losing her job.
12 he had to move house did William realize how much stuff he had/that he had so much stuff.

UNIT 8
Go your own Way

USE OF ENGLISH: Cloze passage
Suggested answers
1 where
2 how
3 play
4 when/while/whilst
5 From
6 with
7 sun
8 not
9 looked
10 down
11 there
12 air/sky
13 to
14 more
15 one
16 if/though
17 what
18 break/split/veer
19 by
20 had

Vocabulary
1
A awe-inspiring
  extraordinary
  amazing
  astonishing
  impressive
  magically

B large group
  jam-packed with
  laden with
  literally thousands of
  sheer concentration
  entire flock
  random swarm
  a scattering
  a gigantic single flying organism
  the flock dispersed

C spiralling
  dipped
  wheeled
  swerving
  turning
  break/split off
  whirling
  swirling
  dance
  dispersed

2 He is painting a picture of the scene with words, trying to give us a feeling both of what he saw and how he felt about it.

3 To make it more interesting, to add emphasis to what he is saying. Using lots of different words can sometimes be more effective than repeating the same words with modifiers, e.g. *Gigantic* can be more effective than *very very big*.

PROVERBS
1
1 E
2 D
3 J
4 C
5 A
6 G
7 I
8 F
9 K
10 B
11 H

2
1 *Birds of a feather flock together.*
   = People with similar ideas and values tend to mix together socially.
2 *Don't count your chickens before they are hatched.*
   = The future is unpredictable so it's dangerous to rely too much on things you think will happen.
3 *Absence makes the heart grow fonder.*
   = We tend to feel a stronger emotional attachment to people when we are separated from them.
4 *Familiarity breeds contempt.*
   = The more familiar we are with things or people, the less we may appreciate them.

ANSWER KEY

5 *Never judge a book by its cover.*
 = Things may not be what they seem at first, first impressions can be misleading.
6 *Don't put all your eggs in one basket.*
 = It is risky to depend totally on one thing.
7 *A bird in the hand is worth two in the bush.*
 = What you have is more valuable than what you may get in the future.
8 *While the cat's away the mice will play.*
 = In the absence of supervision, people may misbehave.
9 *You can lead a horse to water but you can't make it drink.*
 = You can give advice to people, but you can't make them do what they don't want to do.
10 *Finders keepers losers weepers.*
 = We are justified in keeping things we find by chance.
11 *He who laughs last laughs longest.*
 = If you try to get the better of someone, they may end up getting the better of you.

GRAMMAR: Reporting verbs

1 Suggested answers
 1 having eaten/eating so much cake.
 2 his Mum (that) he would send her a postcard as soon as he arrived.
  to send his Mum a postcard as soon as he arrived.
 3 her to go out on her own after dark.
 4 the woman to try a larger size.
  the customer that she should try a larger size.
 5 about the level of noise in the room because/saying he couldn't concentrate.
 6 going home and having a cup of coffee.
  that we/they went home and had a cup of coffee.
  that we/they should go home and have a cup of coffee.
 7 her to take her handkerchief.
 8 that he had been lying to Pauline.
  lying to Pauline.
 9 that (s)he wanted to speak to the manager.
  on speaking to the manager.
 10 to take her son to the cinema.

1 Suggested answers
 1 Lesley phoned Tim to congratulate him on passing his exam.
 2 Peter offered (to give) Linda a lift.
 3 Hugh denied breaking the plate.
  Hugh denied that it was him who had broken the plate.
 4 The owner blamed himself for the failure of the company.
 5 Monica conceded that Gareth had a point.
 6 Penny warned her children not to touch the hot dishes.
 7 Michaela accepted that she had made a serious error of judgement.
 8 Stephen recommended the restaurant in West Street to Kathy.
 9 Suzy's father enquired if/whether she would be staying the night with her grandmother.
 10 Thelma urged Paul to try just one mouthful.

SPELLING

1 A
2 D
3 C
4 D
5 C
6 C
7 A
8 A
9 C
10 D

READING: Gaudy night

Comprehension

1 B
2 C
3 D
4 C
5 D
6 B

Language work

1 If you let people get away with mistakes, then you encourage those who may be dishonest to try and get away with it.
2 something which is right and correct behaviour
3 he is paraphrasing what was said
4 to win an argument or disprove another person's point of view
5 she doesn't seem to understand that some people may be dishonest
6 academic falsification
7 say/do nothing about it
8 that the writer must approve of the young scientists's actions
9 she is not going to name the people she's referring to
10 it didn't really happen, it was invented
11 came across
12 line 40 – an event something which happened
 line 43 – I knew by chance
13 enamoured
14 He might have pretended to find it at a later date, and behave as if he was finding it for the first time.
15 he was not heard of again
16 it wasn't worth it

Wordstress

1 ex<u>ec</u>utive
2 falsifi<u>ca</u>tion
3 manu<u>fac</u>tured
4 <u>ob</u>viously
5 satis<u>fac</u>tion
6 per<u>sua</u>sive
7 <u>eth</u>ical
8 repu<u>ta</u>tion
9 con<u>ten</u>tion
10 <u>pen</u>alize
11 indig<u>na</u>tion
12 contra<u>dic</u>ted
13 de<u>lib</u>erately
14 conside<u>ra</u>tions
15 en<u>am</u>oured
16 cor<u>rect</u>ly
17 person<u>al</u>ities
18 un<u>scru</u>pulous
19 <u>char</u>itable
20 pro<u>fes</u>sorship

USE OF ENGLISH: Gap-fill sentences

1
 1 grown accustomed to
 2 her socks
 3 rid of
 4 cat amongst
 5 as long as
 6 use your trying
 7 help thinking
 8 stand on
 9 as far as
 10 couldn't care
 11 a far cry
 12 a lot to be
 13 once and for
 14 be it from me
 15 on behalf of
 16 burst its
 17 better than
 18 stand much chance

2
 1 took it
 2 a word
 3 brought it
 4 up with
 5 out of
 6 him to
 7 did I
 8 up to
 9 without an
 10 prepared me

ANSWER KEY

UNIT 9
Nose to the Grindstone

VOCABULARY: Wordsearch

1
Horizontal words from the top:
employee, staff, caring, firm, contract, salary, reference, perk, redundancy, boss

Vertical words from the left:
company, job, management, profitable, personnel, business, earnings, efficient, fraud, post, training, competitor, wages, fax, workload, factory, qualifications

2–4

NOUNS	ADJECTIVES
employee	employed
staff	staffed
contract	contractual
salary	salaried
reference	referential
redundancy	redundant
boss	bossy
company	company
management	managerial
personnel	personnel
business	business
earnings	earned
fraud	fraudulent
post	posted
training	trained
wages	waged
competitor	competitive
factory	manufactured
qualifications	qualified
firm	–
job	–
fax	–
workload	–
perk	–

ADJECTIVES	NOUNS
caring	care
efficient	efficiency
profitable	profit

READING:
Mother of all headaches

Pre-reading task

1 neurologist, headaches

2
Para 1 Marcia Wilkinson's background
Para 2 headache sufferers
Para 3 types of headache
Para 4 symptoms of headaches
Para 5 causes of headaches
Para 6 remedies for headaches
Para 7 theories about headaches
Para 8 cure for headaches
Para 9 recent research into headaches
Para 10 prospects for the future

Comprehension
1 B
2 D
3 C
4 D
5 A
6 C

Language work
1 people who have studied headaches
2 he took so many days off that he makes the total look larger
3 ventures, takes a trip
4 courtesy of, sparked off, brought on,
5 no end of
6 they don't know what to do next
7 bewildering
8 there's no saying
9 she's quite an entertaining person, not too serious in her manner, e.g. *when you are hit on the head with a hammer, the greater pain removing the lesser, she breaks into rhyme, this should be stuck up in every physician's consulting room*
10 light-hearted presentation of serious subject matter, e.g. Dr Wilkinson described as *the star* at Federation where she *wowed* the delegates, Alan Frost anecdote, *mother of all headaches, ventures further afield, headless chickens when it comes to headaches, there's no saying whether...*
11 The article is entertaining and, to some extent, informative. It's main purpose is to entertain rather than educate, however.
12 Target reader is probably casual reader in a fairly serious newspaper. Probably a Sunday supplement or similar leisure publication.

GRAMMAR:
Conversational devices

1 Question tags
1 didn't they?
2 doesn't she?
3 are they?
4 won't you?
5 mustn't they?
6 hadn't I?
7 didn't she?
8 wouldn't you?
9 didn't you?
10 had he?
11 didn't it?
12 shouldn't you?
13 do we?
14 wouldn't she?
15 doesn't it?
16 shall we?
17 won't you?
18 haven't I?
19 isn't it?
20 won't you?

2 *So/neither*
1 So does
2 So will
3 So would
4 Nor/Neither are
5 So is
6 Nor/Neither have
7 So does
8 Nor/Neither does
9 Nor/Neither is
10 So did
11 So had
12 Nor/Neither has
13 So might
14 Nor/Neither can
15 Nor/Neither must
16 Nor/Neither ought/should
17 Nor/Neither is
18 Nor/Neither may
19 Nor/Neither is
20 So had

3 Predicative *so/not*
I (don't) believe so, I (don't) suppose so, I (don't) reckon so, I'm afraid so, I presume so, I hope so.
I believe not, I understand not, I hope not, I'm afraid not, I presume not, I suppose not, I guess not, I trust not, I reckon not.

SPELLING:
Commonly misspelled words

1

accom**m**odation	m
exa**g**gerate	g
lit**e**rature	e
busine**ss**man	s
fa**s**cinate	s
disa**p**pearance	p
gover**n**ment	n
disa**pp**ointed	p
im**m**ediately	m
embarra**ss**ed	s
knowledge	k
nece**ss**ity	s
o**p**portunity	p
recom**m**end	m
transfe**r**red	r

2
1 argu**e**ment
2 auxi**l**iary
3 be**g**ginning
4 develop**e**
5 equip**p**ment
6 labo**u**ratory
7 ne**c**cessary
8 occa**s**sionally
9 o**m**mitted
10 paralle**l**
11 personne**l**

109

ANSWER KEY

12 preceede
13 pronounciation
14 responsiability
15 strenghth
16 successfull
17 marketting
18 grammattical

GRAMMAR: Inversion

Suggested answers
1 had Ken put the phone down than it started ringing again.
2 occasion has Robert ever gone against his father's wishes.
3 a day passes without my fiancee and I phoning each other.
4 single plant in the garden survived the heavy frost.
5 to Yvonne's expert advice was the wedding dress finished in time.
6 after years of saving up did the Browns manage to buy their own flat.
7 though/as Tom's lottery winnings were, they were not enough to pay off his debts.
8 did I expect to see Antonietta at Malcom's party.
9 was Ted's hate for his father that he didn't even visit him on his 90th birthday.
10 until he received a letter from his sister that Pete remembered (about) his promise to his family.

USE OF ENGLISH: Cloze passage

Suggested answers
1 be(come)
2 apart
3 in
4 them
5 given
6 and
7 to
8 Getting
9 with
10 off
11 which
12 touch
13 if/whether
14 provided
15 comes
16 takes
17 the
18 up
19 brings
20 taken

UNIT 10
The Road Ahead

VOCABULARY: Multiple choice

1 A
2 C
3 C
4 D
5 D
6 D
7 C
8 B
9 A
10 B

READING:
On four legs you can take forever

Language work
1 He wanted to travel slowly.
2 Other tourists stopped to look at him/treated him as a tourist attraction.
3 They are small and have only basic amenities.
4 supposedly
5 People who know nothing about the subject of horses.
6 That he had begun his trip.
7 hopefully waving a carrot
8 Somebody who knows how to catch the horse, and so helps.
9 trudge/amble
10 a vain bid
11 To show that he wasn't really in control of the horse.
12 To prevent him from falling asleep.

Summary

The summary should include these ideas:
– you may become a tourist attraction
– caravans are small/uncomfortable/ difficult to keep tidy
– you have to learn to control the horse/ caravan
– horses can be very slow/reluctant
– you have to avoid hills/keep to your route

Vocabulary
1 That you needn't have experience of keeping and riding horses.
2 NOUNS: a grey, stable, bridles, bits, collars, saddle, gallop, trot, canter, reins, hooves

   VERBS: stable, saddle, gallop, trot, canter
3 no
4 To give it colour, make it more interesting and involve us in the world of horses. The intended audience is people who haven't had this experience.

Vocabulary: group nouns
1 blanket, duvet, pillow, mattress, quilt, sleeping bag, valence, pillowcase
2 BEDROOM FURNITURE: bedside cabinet, headboard, reading lamp
   SOFT FURNISHINGS: curtain, cushion
   NIGHTWEAR: pyjamas, bedsocks, dressing gown
   CROCKERY: cups, saucers, plates, jugs, bowls, etc.
   CUTLERY: knives, forks, spoons, etc.
   TOILETRIES: soap, toothpaste, shampoo, etc.
   STATIONERY: pens, paper, paper clips, etc.
   SOFT FURNISHINGS: sofa, carpet, curtains, cushions, etc.
3 Yes. e.g. *reading lamp* fits into *bedroom furniture*, *lighting, fixtures and fittings*. *Sleeping bag* is both *bedding* and *camping equipment*.
4 vehicle, kit
5
1 C
2 I
3 D
4 K
5 B
6 H
7 J
8 E
9 G
10 A
11 F

USE OF ENGLISH

Transformation sentences 1:
Suggested answers
1 interested in the job itself as I am in the pay.
2 be going to get that job or you would have heard by now.
3 disappointment of the organizers/organizers' disappointment, only a small number of people attended the conference.
4 as no surprise to me if that company went bankrupt.
5 from the fuchsias, none of the/no plants survived the hard winter.
6 is reported to have left the city early this morning.
7 the impression of someone who's been sitting in the sun all day.
8 Rod grew, the less dependent on his family he became.
9 to stop her pocket money if she disobeyed him.
10 it necessary to water your indoor plants?
11 had the boy recovered from measles than he went down with chicken pox.
12 the fact that she got a bad cough, she wouldn't have given up smoking.

ANSWER KEY

Transformation sentences 2:
Suggested answers
1 David got off to a bad start in the race because he failed to hear the starter's whistle.
2 As long as you remain quiet, you can watch the procession from here.
3 In terms of physical appearance, Henry takes after his father.
4 The car was parked at a distance of 400 metres from the hotel.
5 This old table was handed down to me by my grandmother.
6 Once she had completed the application form, Jill handed it in to the secretary.
7 There were some interesting revelations about a film star in today's newspaper.
8 To sum up, I'd like to make three points.
9 Unless you are in possession of a licence, you can't drive a car.
10 That old market town is worth visiting if you have time.

USE OF ENGLISH: Gap-fill sentences

1 off on
2 the wrong
3 puts his
4 past their
5 known better
6 let you/one
7 fit/no reason
8 owe a

PUNCTUATION

Suggested answers

Ten or eleven years ago, a friend of mine did a counselling course, and she used to come round and tell me about the things they did each week. *I* was fairly uninterested and used to think, *'What* on earth would anyone want to do a course like that for*?'*

However, when my daughter was in her final year of school, and the pressure was on because it was coming up to exam time and she was having difficulties, *I* thought, *'Well* maybe we need some help here.' So *I* rang up the woman who ran the counselling course and my daughter went to see her*.*

What she did, in a very short time*,* was to completely turn things around. *My* daughter went from being someone who wanted to drop out and give up, to someone who was able to face up to things and take responsibility for her own life. And *I* thought, *'That's* amazing! *I* want to know what that woman did.' So *I* signed up for the counselling course myself*.*

SPELLING: Proof reading

1 enspired → inspired
2 mysteriuos → mysterious
3 ninteenth → nineteenth
4 seenic → scenic
5 cities → city's
6 reidetail → residential
7 thoughout → throughout
8 atmosfere → atmosphere
9 wrows → rows
10 concreet → concrete
11 builded → built
12 restaraunt → restaurant
13 arcitecture → architecture
14 comunity → community

USE OF ENGLISH: Cloze test

1 but
2 all
3 sight/crowds
4 although/while/whilst
5 in
6 last
7 of
8 to
9 at
10 before
11 first
12 a
13 one
14 as
15 for
16 accounts
17 who
18 follow
19 if
20 use